CONSULTATION

SCHOOL MENTAL HEALTH PROFESSIONALS AS CONSULTANTS

Don Dinkmeyer, Jr., Ph.D.

Jon Carlson, Psy.D., Ed.D.

Don Dinkmeyer, Sr., Ph.D.

ACCELERATED DEVELOPMENT INC.
PUBLISHERS
MUNCIE, INDIANA

Consultation

School Mental Health Professionals as Consultants

Technical Development: Cynthia Long
Marguerite Mader
Shaeney Pigman
Sheila Sheward

Library of Congress Cataloging-in-Publication Data

Dinkmeyer, Don C., 1952-
    Consultation : school mental health professionals as consultants /
Don Dinkmeyer, Jr., Jon Carlson, Don Dinkmeyer, Sr.
      p. cm.
    Includes bibliographical references and index.
    ISBN 1-55959-036-X
    1. School children—Mental health services. 2. Mental health
consultation.   3. Student counselors. 4. Adlerian psychology.
5. Educational counseling. I. Carlson, Jon. II. Dinkmeyer, Don C.
III. Title.
    [DNLM: 1. Referral and Consultation. 2. Psychological Theory.
3. Counseling—methods. 4. School Health Services—United States.
5. Mental Health Services—United States. WM 55 D585c 1993]
LB3430.D56 1993
  371.7'13—dc20
DNLM/DLC
for Library of Congress   93-13252
                                        CIP

LCN: 93-13252
ISBN:1-55959-036-X

Order additional copies from:

ACCELERATED DEVELOPMENT INC., Publishers
3808 West Kilgore Avenue
Muncie, Indiana 47304-4896
(317) 284-7511
Toll Free Order Number 1-800-222-1166

DEDICATION

To Joe Hollis

for his dedication to Individual Psychology

and ability to spread the ideas through many good books.

ACKNOWLEDGEMENTS

We are grateful to the graduate students at Governors State University, University Park, Illinois for a detailed critique of the book. Thanks are also expressed to Candace Ward Howell, Cindy Runnells, Nancy Richards, and Mary Bregman for their help on this project.

We also express appreciation to Joe Hollis of Accelerated Development for his unflagging commitment to this project. His encouragement and understanding during the long process of writing this book were crucial to our efforts.

vi Consultation

FOREWORD

Could it be that Dinkmeyer, Carlson, and Dinkmeyer have come up with a very practical approach to consultation? Could it also be that they have taken one specific theory of human development and personality and demonstrated its practical use for consultation? If after you read this book you answer "yes" to these two questions, then you will agree with me that this book is a valuable contribution to the ever-growing practice of consultation.

Unlike most books on this subject, which globally define consultation and outline various models (e.g., mental health, behavioral, organizational), this book zeroes in on one specific model based on Adlerian or Individual Psychology. Consequently a greater depth of understanding can be acquired regarding a single effective approach to consultation.

These authors published their original book on consulting when the term "consultation" and accompanying practices were early in development. This second edition addresses the subject at its current level of sophistication, which is a far cry from where it was in 1973. In fact, counseling in general and particularly school counseling have evolved many fold since the first edition of this book was published. For example, a very sophisticated credentialing process has been established from training standards to licensure of counselors. As of the first printing of this book, no states had counseling licensure boards. Although all states have some form of school counselor certification, now some 38 states plus the District of Columbia have licensure, registry, or certification of professional counselors. Another relatively new credential is offered through the National Board for Certified Counselors (NBCC) with specialty certification in identified areas. A national exam has been developed, administered, and normed for use by both the NBCC and most state licensure boards.

A set of rigorous training standards has been adopted by the American Association for Counseling and Development and administered through the Council for Accreditation of Counseling and Related Educational Programs (CACREP). These standards have been applied to counselor education programs in colleges and universities throughout the country with approximately 70 accredited programs to date. These standards require a minimum of two years of full-time graduate study, including extensive supervised practicum and internship experience. Eight common-core areas with accompanying knowledge and skill competencies are within the standards. Included within these required competencies is the area of consultation. When this book was first published very few counselor education programs required a course in consultation, let alone offered one as an elective. Now with these standards for preparation, consultation skills are virtually guaranteed through these CACREP-approved programs.

Education also has come a long way since the authors' first publication on consulting. A plethora of studies and subsequent legislation has addressed education in the United States. Considerable pressure has been placed on the educational community to show results of their efforts. Through this emphasis and study of education and the learning process the lay community has become better educated. Many have recognized that education is more than a cognitive activity; others have dug in their heels and pressured schools to focus only on the three Rs. In some cases this increased awareness has provided the stimulus for the need for expanded counseling services. In fact, counseling has emerged in many places as the key to addressing many societal ills as a result of the flushing out of many problems such as high dropout rates, teen pregnancy, AIDS, substance abuse, childhood hunger, to name a few. This pressure has forced many counselors to rethink their role and develop the consultation skills necessary to address new demands on them.

Yes, consultation has come a long way since 1973. This new book has been long overdue. I congratulate the authors for taking the time to create this new volume and share their talents with us.

As pointed out in Chapter 1, the book is divided into eight chapters, with Chapter 1 establishing the rationale and overview of consultation. Chapter 2 addresses the consultant's role and general processes with an emphasis on the critical need for establishing a working relationship with the consultee. In Chapter 3 you will find a discussion of the authors' orientation to consultation which is grounded in Individual Psychology. For a good overview of this theory, a wise procedure would be to read Chapter 7 first. Although the chapter addresses consultation with parents and families, it provides a quick refresher of Adlerian psychology. The remaining chapters of the book address consultation as applied to specific settings and populations. Finally, Chapter 8 offers an extensive set of case studies demonstrating the theory and process of consultation as addressed in the book.

This book is must reading for counselors with an Adlerian orientation to the field. It is the only book of which I am aware that takes Adlerian Psychology and applies the theory to consultation practices.

Joseph C. Rotter
Professor, Counselor Education
University of South Carolina

PREFACE

This book is for school personnel who work with teachers, students, parents, and administrators in our school systems. We believe the school counselor is the individual most likely to play this role. All four populations expect the counselor to serve them, and consultation is an effective means to meeting their needs. A consultation approach is often the relationship of choice.

Consultation: School Mental Health Professionals as Consultants gives mental health professionals a set of skills for working with these populations. We have focused on a skill in each chapter and expect the reader to be unfamiliar with many of our ideas. These ideas come from Individual Psychology (IP), and we are grateful to those who preceded our works in this field of psychology. IP has a rich tradition of working in the schools and with parents. This book represents a new synthesis of the ideas for all of the school populations.

We bring more than 75 years of experience, including work in literally all 50 states, Canada, and internationally to this book. Wherever we teach, we are increasingly impressed with both the severity and similarity of the needs. Although our schools are increasingly challenged to meet the needs of our society, we believe they are a major influence on the way generations are learning to cooperate, collaborate, and compete. This book is our effort to help you become a more effective school consultant.

Don Dinkmeyer, Jr.
Jon Carlson
Don Dinkmeyer, Sr.

CONTENTS

Chapter **1**

INTRODUCTION AND OVERVIEW

In this chapter you will learn:

- how changing society/school necessitates a consultant's role,
- the importance of creating a more humane society,
- how we learn and why that is important,
- the importance of self-esteem,
- the value of consulting,
- three components of consulting, and
- guidelines and effectiveness of consulting in schools.

Consulting was more a dream than a reality when we wrote *Consulting: Facilitating Humaneness and Change Processes* (Dinkmeyer & Carlson, 1973). Counselors talked about doing counseling, consulting, and coordination, but few actually understood what effective consultation entailed. Since this inaugural volume, counselors and counselor educators have become aware of the power and effectiveness of effective consultation. Research studies continue (for over 30 years) to show the power of effective consulting, but counselors still do not use these methods at an effective level. Why?

We believe that a clear statement has not existed for school consultants prior to this book. Our ideas have been developed from working at all school levels for over 30 years. The approach is skill-based and has its roots in Adlerian or Individual Psychology. Adlerian psychology is a goal-directed approach that believes that people have choices and that therapy needs to build on individuals' strengths. This approach is holistic and focuses upon the total system or milieu. Our ideas have influenced millions through these educational programs.

For Students

DUSO (Developing Understanding of Self and Others) I and II. Dinkmeyer & Dinkmeyer. 1982.

Drug Free: A DUSO Approach to Preventing Drug Abuse. McKay, Dinkmeyer, & Dinkmeyer. 1989.

PREP for Effective Family Living. Dinkmeyer, McKay, Dinkmeyer, Dinkmeyer, & Carlson. 1985.

For Teachers

STET (Systematic Training for Effective Teaching). Dinkmeyer, McKay, & Dinkmeyer. 1980.

Teaching and Leading Children. Dinkmeyer, McKay, Dinkmeyer, & Dinkmeyer. 1993.

For Parents

STEP (Systematic Training for Effective Parenting). Dinkmeyer & McKay. 1989.

STEP/TEEN (Systematic Training for Effective Parenting of Teens). Dinkmeyer & McKay. 1990.

The Next STEP. Dinkmeyer, McKay, Dinkmeyer, Dinkmeyer, & McKay. 1987.

Early Childhood STEP. Dinkmeyer, McKay, & Dinkmeyer. 1989.

For Couples

TIME (Training in Marriage Enrichment). Dinkmeyer & Carlson. 1984.

CONSULTATION GUIDELINES

This book has been written to provide specific guidelines for counselors on how to use consultation in the schools. We emphasize the following five themes.

1. The consultant is often a school counselor.

2. Every consultant has a specific set of beliefs about human behavior.

3. An effective consultation theory is necessary.

4. Consultants must be able to take broad knowledge and create specific practical consultation strategies.

5. Case studies and commentary can increase your consulting skills.

1. The Consultant Is Often a School Counselor.

Although others will benefit from this book, the authors recognize counselors are frequently asked to serve as consultants. Counselors have definite advantages and disadvantages when consulting in the schools. Many other professionals also may be consultants—school psychologists, social workers, special education teachers, practicum students, and others. This book is equally appropriate for these individuals. The counselor's role as a consultant is presented in Chapter 2.

2. Every Consultant Has a Specific Set of Beliefs about Human Behavior.

Your beliefs about behavior have a strong influence on your consulting abilities. The key to effective consultation is an effective practical understanding of behavior, motivation, and discipline. In this book you will be asked to expand beliefs and thereby increase skills.

3. An Effective Consultation Theory Is Necessary.

Our theoretical approach is presented in Chapter 3. Our assumptions are based in Individual or Adlerian Psychology. The Adlerian approach complements and integrates the other theories of consultation.

4. Consultants Must Be Able to Take Broad Knowledge and Create Specific Practical Consultation Strategies.

The ability to create or "tailor" strategies to specific situations is the hallmark of effective consulting. Specific techniques for working with teachers, students, and parents are presented in Chapters 4 through 7.

5. Case Studies and Commentary Can Increase Your Consulting Skills.

Consultation cases are presented, followed by critiques from the authors. These appear in Chapter 8.

Consultants need to operate systemically and to understand the environment and the environmental influences on the teachers, parents, administrators, and students. Society has changed, and though many of the changes seem beneficial, they have a tendency to dehumanize people. In the following section, we will look at how society has changed, the importance of meaningful learning, and how self-esteem is a key ingredient in learning and growing.

SOCIETY HAS CHANGED

Schools do not operate in a vacuum. They reflect America's efforts in the 1990s to prepare future adults. Therefore, to examine recent changes in our society is significant and relevant.

Fundamental and substantial changes have occurred in the past quarter century. Passive acceptance of autocratic procedures and unequal treatment of women, minorities, and children are no longer unquestioned. Pressure to institute democratic procedures in the classroom indicates that autocratic procedures are less effective. Demands for compliance are less successful than efforts to cooperate. A profound and widespread change has occurred in our society. The school consultant must be aware of this change.

In the 1950s, our society could be characterized as **autocratic**. A few people were in charge and all others were expected to obey. In the family, fathers were often in charge. In schools, the teacher was in control of the classroom. The society shifted from an autocracy to a permissive orientation as labor, women, minorities, and others asserted their rights. The autocrats lost control. In the family, parents tried to give their children "everything we didn't have as kids," but this often meant the giving of material possessions and creating dependence. Although these "good" parents were well-meaning, their efforts often created more harm than responsible growth. Many of our solutions are short-term satisfying and long-term unhealthy because in today's drive-through fast-paced society, we seldom look at the longer-term implications of our actions.

The **permissive** society did not solve many problems. It confused equality with entitlement. The shift in parent-child and teacher-student relationships can be shown in the following example. Many times in the past when an adult said, "jump," the child would say, "how high?" Now when an adult says, "jump," the child says, "why?" or "go jump yourself."

We do not advocate autocratic or permissive relationships. **Democratic** relationships are more effective; however, often are not practiced. In democratic relationships, children are taught both freedom and responsibility. Many are confused by what this entails. In a democratic relationship, someone is in charge. The person in charge guides others through choice-making and encouragement. Consultants need to be personally aware of this process in order to bring about change themselves and to guide others in order to create a democratic system.

Children cannot learn about democracy vicariously; they must live it. However, teachers cannot be free to practice democracy in the classroom if they fear autocratic supervisors who are not trained in group procedures which enable them to provide democratic leadership or if they have unequal primary (marital) relationships.

The society has reacted to the preceding changes by placing more demands on staff and students. We now have vastly increased *knowledge* about many subjects, but we have failed to recognize that the increase in knowledge was not accompanied by a commensurate increase in learning capacity on the part of students nor in the ability to realize effectively how this information can be of use or processed in daily life. The teacher is no longer primarily a dispenser of knowledge, secure in the belief that the students are motivated and able to learn.

A close inspection of educational practices and methods indicates a great disparity between objectives and what is actually accomplished. Unlike business which fires the unsuccessful salesperson, schools believe that when the teacher does not "sell" or motivate the child, the child is the failure. The teacher's responsibility is to teach and to take responsibility for helping each individual to learn. Most children seem to follow a prescribed path, while others need individually guided instruction. We have difficulty in believing that children are ever failures and therefore we must take responsibility and strive to help them learn.

The single most important characteristic that our schools often share is a preoccupation with order and control. Teachers become disciplinarians with a goal of the absence of noise and movement. We insist that children sit silent and motionless, which is quite unnatural. We also assume that all students will be interested in the same thing at the same moment for the same length of time. Educators often expect "smudgeless" carbon copies of the "ideal" student.

Our economic and political systems appear to reward material gains over human values. Social responsibility, spiritual values, and character are discussed and verbally lauded, but they are not prized and rewarded. Additionally, teachers and parents do not model what they preach (Carlson & Thorpe, 1984). Material values push people to compete in an unending, unrewarding battle to have more than others. Individuals are engaged in talking about equality while demonstrating inequality at all levels. The administrator feels superior to the teacher, the teacher feels superior to the parent, the parent feels superior to the child, and the child struggles to get rights. From all of this emerges the "getting" person, one concerned about what he or she can accomplish for self while remaining unconcerned about others.

Schools are often more concerned with whether children know the correct answers to the 8th grade Constitution test rather than whether they have an experience in democratic living within the classroom. In practice, our goals and objectives appear to be limited to acquiring facts. We tell children that democracy, cooperation, peace, and brotherhood are the goals of a happy and successful life. Yet, we introduce, train for, and demonstrate these concepts in an authoritarian and competitive manner (i.e., getting ahead at the expense of others), the direct opposite of the stated objectives or eventual goals. Students learn from what we do rather than from what we say. The model of the benevolent autocrat who fosters competition is internalized.

We must meet the challenge of our times to live truly as equals. This recognizes that we are equal in value even though we might not be equal in social position. The basic social conflict involves a struggle for control, the over-ambition to be more than others, and the resultant nagging feeling of inadequacy and alienation. The challenge is clear: we must learn to live as equals. Equality does not mean equal intelligence, responsibility, or commitment. It means the ability to treat each other with respect.

The revolution against authority and autocratic methods has created the basic shift in our culture. Consultants must become familiar with democratic procedures. The democratic system is not faulty, but we have people attempting to operate the system who have not learned how to function democratically. Their experiences at home and at school have trained them to deal with superior-inferior relationships, not to live as equals. Democratic procedures require that each person must *choose*, become responsible for his/her own behavior, and as a result be in control of self. Each person is a social equal in a democratic society. However, some people do need to take control and be in charge.

THE IMPORTANCE OF LEARNING

Two components of learning are information and meaning. We have more information than we need. When we fail, it is because we have not discovered the meaning of the information we have. Nothing is learned until it has become personally meaningful and it actually influences our perceptions and behavior. We know we should listen to feelings and beliefs of our students, but we have so many "pages to cover." We clearly have not learned the importance of listening.

Teachers do not fail because they do not know their subject matter. They fail because they are unable in one way or another to make this information meaningful. The information component of the learning process lies *outside* the learner and because of this other people can do something about it. However, the meaning aspect lies *within* the learner and is not so open for us to change. But educators want to change by altering the information component. This is the main aspect of the learning process with which teachers are attempting to directly modify and influence.

The rationale follows along these lines. If a little information is a good thing, then a whole lot must be a whole lot better. Subsequently, we are drowning kids in information with the following approaches:

- longer days at school;
- fewer vacations;
- more courses;
- less physical education or anything considered a frill such as music, drama, or art; and
- foreign languages in the elementary school and more math and science.

Most of us do not need more information. More important than the giving of information is helping people to understand the personal meaning of the information. Dropouts or school failures did not quit because of a lack of information. Everybody offered them that. They were not, however, helped to see the relationship between the information and their personal needs. Involvement and meaning were not developed. A big difference exists between knowing and behaving. Knowing results from acquiring new information. A change in behavior comes with the discovery of meaning.

Children need to feel safe and secure before they can feel challenged. If they are not safe, they feel threatened. Threat deters learning, while challenge fosters learning. Yet we continue to threaten children in order to motivate (e.g., grades, no recess, *"I'll send a note home."*).

We must dispel the depersonalization that is impinging on human needs. We can no longer rationalize these dilemmas with such statements as, *"Maybe things are not so bad after all."* This is the kind of defense mechanism that has helped us to reach our present state. (What rationalizations have you developed for why you and your school are not functioning this way?)

The evolution of the humane person requires changes in education, changes as radical as the technological shifts of the past decade. These changes will require boldness, imagination, and hard work. Wishing will not bring them about. Change requires optimism and a belief in the intrinsic worth of each person. Change requires changing the people who set the policy, make the decisions, and facilitate the growth of students. This change can occur only by dealing with the person's beliefs. Traditional change processes and in-service programs have exposed the populace to ideas and concepts, but have not permitted the person to internalize these concepts in terms of personal attitudes and beliefs.

Education should prepare people not just to make or earn a living, but to live a creative, humane, and sensitive life. The purpose of education is to turn out men and women who are capable of educating their friends, their communities, and, most importantly, themselves. Education is *not* a spectator sport. It is life, and each individual needs to get involved.

The problem is larger, as Rudolf Dreikurs (1971) indicated when he stated that

> today husband and wife cannot live separately with each other if they do not treat each other as equals. Nor can parents get along with their children if they assume that children can be subdued. There can be

no harmony and stability in the community unless each member of it has his safe place as an equal to all others. There can be no cooperation between management and labor unless each group feels respected and trusted by the other. There can be no peace on earth unless one nation respects the rights and dignity of another. (p. xiii)

SELF-ESTEEM

Self-esteem, or believing you are of value, is the key trait in being able to live as equals. A number of factors in schools have a negative influence upon self-concept and self-esteem. As one passes through school, an increasing emphasis is placed upon memorizing (despite teachers professing to reinforce creative, curious, and spontaneous children) if one is to achieve the typical rewards of the school. This is accompanied by the fact that education unfortunately becomes increasingly less relevant for the child's personal and social needs.

Schools also discourage students from developing the capacity to learn by and for themselves because schools are structured in such a way as to make students totally dependent upon teachers. Students' curiosity, spontaneity, and courage are not reinforced. Their ability and desire to think and act for themselves are diminished rather than increased.

A stated educational goal is to help children to develop responsibility for the direction of their lives. In our society, we do not let children assume responsibility for their future until they reach the late teenage years. At that time they are expected to make reasonable decisions and choices. Upon completion of high school, for example, children are required to choose their vocation or attend and graduate from college. Yet prior to this time they have had little training and no experience in decision making, often having parents that still wake them up in the morning, remind them to do their homework, and provide other unnecessary services, thus, a high college dropout rate, divorce rate, and considerable vocational transfer. Many high school districts graduate only approximately 50% of their students. This suggests education is a random chance series of events which guarantees equal doses of failure and success.

A child cannot become successful by learning only from the experience of others. In order to become successful, one must establish anchors and contact with a personal reality. The student must begin to get involved and to evaluate his/her performance. Teachers don't have to evaluate everything a child does.

The knowledge explosion had a tremendous impact upon American education. The launching of the Russian Sputnik in 1957 is recognized as the date when the United States first felt challenged by the scientific achievement of other cultures. What became increasingly apparent was that a greater amount of information was available than one could readily master through traditional methods. Thus, we were at a turning point where we had to decide whether we should emphasize facts and information or instead attitudes.

The decision was made to place an emphasis upon acquiring knowledge. This resulted in the placement of college subjects into the high school curricula and the moving of high school subjects to the elementary level. One might only speculate on the results if instead we had abandoned any attempt to master all the current knowledge, which is being outdated rapidly by scientific research, and had focused on developing positive attitudes towards learning and a desire to become involved in the educational process as a lifetime task.

If education is to stress humaneness, a systematic emphasis must be in the following areas.

1. New life patterns emerging in response to changing knowledge and technology will require schools and colleges to function decreasingly as primary sources of knowledge and increasingly as developers of capacities to process information and reorganize experiences obtained in family, community, work situations, and a variety of complementary institutions.

2. Vigorous measures are needed to strengthen the knowledge base from which education operates. The emphasis needs to be on making current information meaningful rather than on giving more information.

3. Greatly increased effort must be directed to establishing the essential preconditions for effective learning.

4. Continuous curriculum adaptation is necessary in order to receive new inputs which reflect (a) the current state of knowledge in each subject of instruction, and (b) the behavioral knowledge applicable to teaching and learning.

5. Education needs better processes for helping individuals to order their values so as to help them make better choices as to how their energies and eventually their lives are spent.

WHY CONSULTATION?

The need for counselors to be skilled in consultation has been clearly articulated (Brown, Spano, & Schulte, 1988; Drapela, 1985; Nelson & Shifron, 1985; Umansky & Holloway, 1984), and the profession has responded. The Council for Accreditation of Counseling and Related Educational Programs (1988) has included a requirement for curricular experience in the theories and applications of consultation in its standards for accreditation for graduate programs. The American School Counselor Association (1986) has included competencies in consultation in its professional development guidelines for secondary school counselors, and the Association for Counselor Education and Supervision has published two handbooks on consultation (Brown, Kurpius, & Morris, 1988; Kurpius & Brown, 1988). Although it is deemed critical that counseling students receive training in consultation, research suggests that many counselor education programs provide only minimal education in this area and that students are graduating without proper preparation in consultation (Brown, Spano, & Schulte, 1988). A need exists for the development of innovative strategies to convey the basic principles and techniques of consultation.

Consultation offers counselors a powerful tool to change the school environment and community. Reynolds, Gutkin, Elliot, and Witt (1984) summarized the literature that compared the effectiveness of consulting with that of counseling. The research supported the fact that consulting was much more time efficient and therefore cost effective. The counselor who works with one client impacts one person and his or her life. The consultant who works with one teacher indirectly affects the lives of 30 or more children. The consultant who works with one parent education group may affect the lives of 20 to 30 children.

With this rationale in mind, we have chosen to work with those who have the largest impact on the school system. Additionally, usually teachers, parents, and administrators are the ones who identify problems and are invested in seeing that they change. Additionally, if the parent or teacher changes, then changing the student is easier. Often students have little motivation to change.

Counselors are able to help students to function more effectively in their environments, while consultants are more likely to change the environment. Parents are taught to teach their children social skills and to create home environments where children can flourish socially, emotionally, and intellectually. Teachers can learn to create a similar environment and administrators are helped to develop a system where human needs are of the highest priority.

According to Brown, Kurpius, and Morris (1988),

> Through consultation, primary prevention programs can be developed that will contribute to work, family, and educational environments that will be less likely to contribute to dysfunctional living. Parents who learn to deal with an under-achieving child may be better able to prevent that syndrome in future with their other children. Employers who inadvertently create stressful environments may be able to increase commitment and reduce absenteeism, tardiness, and reduce health care costs simply by restructuring the work place. Consultants

have helped teachers, parents, employees, and others become effective agents against mental health problems. (p. 7)

CONSULTATION DEFINED

Each consultation has three parties: the consultant, the consultee, and the client or problem. Broad generalizations can be made about each. In Figure 1.1 are shown the three parties and the relationship among them.

Consultants can be any individual asked to intervene in a situation in which a consultee and problem exist. Consultants are skilled at understanding consultees and their problems.

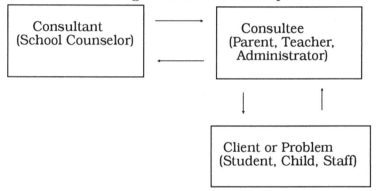

Figure 1.1. The consultant, the consultee, and the child or problem and the relationship among them.

The **consultee** typically brings the problem to the first meeting. Consultees are often teachers, parents, or administrators.

The **problem** is either a person or a situation, sometimes both. For example, a consultee (teacher) may come with a problem (a specific student) or a consultee (principal) may come with a problem (lack of discipline in most classrooms).

Most consultation situations involve adults attempting to change adult-student relationships. Students are not directly involved in the consultation.

Consultation involves sharing information, ideas; coordinating, comparing observations; providing a sounding board; and developing tentative hypotheses for action. The emphasis is on equal relationships developed through collaboration and joint planning. This is to be distinguished from the superior-inferior consulting relationships where the consultant is the only expert. The purpose is to develop tentative recommendations which fit the uniqueness of the child, the teacher, the parent, and the setting.

Consultation relationships have the following four characteristics.

1. Information, observations, and concerns about a problem are **shared** between the consultant and the consultee.

2. **Tentative hypotheses** are developed to change the situation.

3. Joint **planning and collaboration** occur between consultant and consultee.

4. The hypotheses, or recommendations, **reflect** and **respect** the uniqueness of the child, the teacher, and the setting.

These four points emphasize the equality of the relationship between the consultee and consultant. A widespread faulty belief about school consultation relationships is that teachers send students to consultants to be "fixed." This is not a consultation relationship. It is a myth! The problem is in the relationship system of teacher and student. Let's examine the implications of the characteristics.

Sharing Information

The school consultant is able to bring new ideas to the consultee. The consultant teaches the consultee skills and a systematic approach for solving similar problems in the future. Information concerning behavior, misbehavior, group dynamics, teachers' beliefs, discipline procedures, and motivation techniques are all part of the consultant's repertoire. In Chapter 4 we present this information and make suggestions on the most appropriate teaching methods in the consultation relationship.

The primary characteristic of the consultant's information is that it is consistent with a theory of human behavior that the consultant thinks will help the consultee. We can summarize our approach by stating that the behavior, even misbehavior, has a purpose which can be understood (Dreikurs, 1950). Further, the most effective techniques for change require the consultee, the person most interested in change, to initiate new behaviors (i.e., show how the teacher needs to change first).

Providing a Sounding Board

Most consultants have been trained in counseling and listening skills. When the consultee presents a situation, a critical point is that effective listening precede any new information. Effective consultants must be capable of focused and reflective listening. Being able to do so is a cornerstone skill in counseling and equally important in consultation. Additionally, the consultant goes beyond listening and facilitates understanding of the dynamics of behavior through effective questions.

Maintaining an Equal Relationship

A superior to inferior relationship suggests that consultees seek advice which consultants eagerly dispense. Instead, we advocate an equal relationship. Equality means the consultant is not an expert dispensing advice on demand. The consultee has equal responsibility for changing the situation which prompts the consultation relationship. This perspective on the consulting relationship is different from traditional and widespread beliefs about the consultant's role in the schools.

Changing Both Beliefs and Behavior

Consultants realize that unless concrete action takes place as a result of the consultation meeting, nothing has changed. The consultant operates not as an expert suggestion dispenser, but rather a facilitator who helps the consultee to develop workable recommendations. The consultant need not feel totally comfortable nor committed about the recommendations the consultee develops. Recommendations that are not effective will be assessed at the next meeting and alternatives developed. An important point to remember is that recommendations are not just about behavior, but also deal specifically with the beliefs of the consultee. For example, Karin tries to sleep during her first two classes each day. Karin's teacher believes that she comes from a home with minimal parental guidance and is really tired. This belief prevented the teacher from understanding her role in this behavior. Karin was actually using this behavior for attention and to find her place in the classroom.

INEFFECTIVE ROLES VERSUS EFFECTIVE ROLES

The consultant's role needs to be clearly understood by teachers, parents, and administrators. Others must be educated as to how this role differs from traditional counseling roles. Requests from teachers, administrators, and parents may create ineffective consultation relationships. Effective consultation is not simply responding to a sometimes confusing and demanding set of requests. Consider the following examples.

Mrs. Page, a third grade teacher, frequently sends students to the counselor. She reports that students are disrupting the classroom and would benefit from special attention by the counselor.

The principal asks the counselor to become part of the school's discipline system. Any student sent to the office twice in one week must see the counselor.

The mother of a second grader is concerned that her son will be asked to repeat that grade unless he shows improvement. Can the counselor talk to the teacher or principal or both?

These three situations could easily become ineffective consultation situations. The consultant must understand the underlying belief each person has about the nature of change. In each of these situations, the person (consultee) believes the counselor (consultant) will solve the problem. Perhaps the most widespread, ineffective problem-solving belief is "fix the child."

Consultants understand the importance of problem ownership. If a consultee comes to the consultant with a problem, the consultee owns the problem and needs to be helped with the problem. However, when a consultant sees a situation that she/he finds unacceptable, then the consultant owns the problem and must initiate the action and take responsibility for the change. In the previous example with Mrs. Page, the consultant would need to work with Mrs. Page and help her understand just how the children are a problem for her and what she might do differently. The principal in the previous example needs to understand how discipline is the responsibility of the teacher or administrator in charge and to take the student out of the situation to talk with the counselor does little to change the existing system. Finally, with the concerned mother, the consultant needs to help her to learn how to deal effectively with her child and the significant adults in her child's world.

Counselors often have students referred to them. The referring teachers are generally friendly and cooperative, as they expect you, the consultant, to solve their problem. The counselor is expected to help the student who often does not see the problem or feel a need to change. Without the readiness or need to change present, the counselor is at a big disadvantage.

However, by working with the referring teacher, the consultant can become effective. The teacher is upset and in a state of dissonance (Festinger, 1957). He/she has a problem and wants it solved. By helping the teacher to own the problem and take responsibility for its resolution, the disadvantage is gone. The one who wants change can create it. The one who needs help will get it, and the one who wants the help is able to help self.

School counselors are not consultants when they act as a referral service for misbehaving students. Unless the teacher is equally involved in the process, the process is not consultation. Recent writers in the field of consultation clearly show how consultation works in the school setting. However, no one broad or universally accepted definition of consultation has been accepted (Brown, Kurpius, & Morris, 1988; Dougherty, 1990; Hansen, Himes, & Meier, 1990).

The **setting** for consultation began in hospitals and mental health clinics where medical personnel asked for additional services in solving medical problems. This approach, asking for help to solve problems, spread to industry, community agencies, and schools.

The **role** of a consultant depends on the services provided. Schein (1969) described an "expert" consultation role in which the consultant solves the problems. For example, the patient with a skin condition is referred to a dermatologist because the family physician cannot diagnose the condition. The dermatologist (consultant) identifies the condition and prescribes the remedy.

Another consultation role more closely identified with school counselors is the prescriptive mode. The consultant gathers information, identifies the problem, and then tells the consultee what steps should be taken (Kurpius & Brubaker, 1976). The role resembles the medical doctor because the consultant unilaterally reaches the solution and then offers it to the consultee.

The role that most clearly resembles ours is that of a collaborator, one who forms egalitarian relationships with the consultees in order to help them change. In this relationship, a joint diagnosis occurs with a focus on helping consultees to develop their own solutions. The consultant serves as a facilitator of the problem-solving process. This role allows the consultee to develop skills and to not be dependent on the consultant.

Skills for consultation must include the traditional initial relationship skills such as **attending** and **listening,** as well as the **ability to assess problems**.

No single theory is identified with consultation. Kurpius and Robinson (1978) stated that the consultant is guided by the philosophy he/she believes can most efficiently and effectively change the system.

The process of consultation consists of discrete steps which move from building a relationship to evaluating the outcome. The objectives of the consultation serve as the framework for evaluating the outcome.

CONCLUSION

A systematic provision for consultation in schools is advocated. The consultant utilizes skills in **interpersonal relationships, learning processes**, and **group procedures** to facilitate the development of the helping relationship between staff members and students.

We will present a theory of human behavior that facilitates more effective human relationships. It includes a theoretical rationale for the consultant as a specialist in human relationships; the theory and practice of consulting with teachers, administrators, and parents; and practical examples of work with individuals and groups. The classroom as well as the system as a whole are discussed and methods for releasing their inherent human potential are presented.

REVIEW QUESTIONS

1. How have changes from autocratic to democratic living affected society in general and schools specifically?

2. What are the characteristics of a democratic relationship?

3. Do you believe people can really live as equals?

4. How can consultants help teachers learn to make learning more meaningful?

5. Describe how schools discourage students and create low self-esteem.

6. What is meant by humaneness and how can schools really create humane environments?

7. How would you develop a rationale for consulting in the schools?

8. What are the four characteristics of a consultation relationship?

9. How would you define consultation?

REFERENCES

American School Counselor Association. (1986). *Professional development guidelines for secondary school counselors: A self-audit.* Alexandria, VA: Author.

Brown, D., Kurpius, D. J., & Morris, J. R. (1988). *Handbook of consultation with individuals and small groups.* Alexandria, VA: Association for Counselor Education and Supervision.

Brown, D., Spano, D. B., & Schulte, A. C. (1988). Consultation training in master's level counselor education programs. *Counselor Education and Supervision, 27,* 323-330.

Carlson, J., & Thorpe, C. (1984). *The growing teacher.* Engelwood Cliffs, NJ: Prentice Hall.

Council for Accreditation of Counseling and Related Educational Programs. (1988). Accreditation standards of the Council for Accreditation of Counseling and Related Educational Programs. Alexandria, VA: Author.

Dinkmeyer, D., & Carlson, J. (1973). *Consulting: Facilitating human potential and change processes.* Columbus, OH: Charles Merrill.

Dinkmeyer, D., & Carlson, J. (1984). *Training in marriage enrichment* (TIME). Circle Pines, MN: American Guidance Service.

Dinkmeyer, D., & Dinkmeyer, D., Jr. (1982). *Developing understanding of self and others* (DUSO). I and II. Circle Pines, MN: American Guidance Service.

Dinkmeyer, D., & McKay, G. (1989). *Systematic training for effective parenting* (STEP). Circle Pines, MN: American Guidance Service.

Dinkmeyer, D., & McKay, G. (1990). *Systematic training for effective parenting of teenagers (STEP/TEEN).* Circle Pines, MN: American Guidance Service.

Dinkmeyer, D., McKay, G., & Dinkmeyer, D., Jr. (1980). *Systematic training for effective teaching* (STET). Circle Pines, MN: American Guidance Service.

Dinkmeyer, D., McKay, G., & Dinkmeyer, J. (1989). *Early childhood STEP.* Circle Pines, MN: American Guidance Service.

Dinkmeyer, D., McKay, G., Dinkmeyer, D., Jr., Dinkmeyer, J., & Carlson, J. (1985). *PREP for effective family living.* Circle Pines, MN: American Guidance Service.

Dinkmeyer, D., McKay, G., Dinkmeyer, D., Jr., Dinkmeyer, J., & McKay, J. (1987). *The Next STEP.* Circle Pines, MN: American Guidance Service.

Dinkmeyer, D., MaKay, G., Dinkmeyer, D., Jr., & Dinkmeyer, J. (1993). *Teaching and leading children.* Circle Pines, MN: American Guidance Service.

Dougherty, A. M. (1990). *Consultation: Practice and perspectives.* Belmont, CA: Wadsworth.

Drapela, V. J. (1985). An integrative approach to teaching consultation and supervision. *Counselor Education and Supervision, 24,* 341-348.

Dreikurs, R. (1950). *Fundamentals of Adlerian psychology.* Chicago: Alfred Adler Institute.

Dreikurs, R. (1971). *Social equality: The challenge of today.* Chicago: Alfred Adler Institute.

Festinger, L. (1957). *A theory of cognitive dissonance.* Stanford, CA: Stanford University Press.

Hansen, J. C., Himes, B. S., & Meier, S. (1990). *Consultation: Concepts and practices.* Engelwood Cliffs, NJ: Prentice Hall.

Kurpius, D. J., & Brown, D. (1988). *Handbook of consultation: An intervention for advocacy and outreach.* Alexandria, VA: Association for Counselor Education and Supervision.

Kurpius, D. J., & Brubaker, J. C. (1976). *Psycho-educational consultation: Definition—function—preparation.* Bloomington, IN: Indiana University.

Kurpius, D. J., & Robinson, S. E. (1978). An overview of consultation. *Personnel and Guidance Journal,* 56 (6), 321-323.

McKay, J., Dinkmeyer, D., & Dinkmeyer, D., Jr. (1989). *Drug free: A DUSO approach to preventing drug abuse.* Circle Pines, MN: American Guidance Service.

Nelson, R. C., & Shifron, R. (1985). Choice awareness in consultation. *Counselor Education and Supervision, 24,* 298-306.

Reynolds, C. R., Gutkin, T. B., Elliot, S. N., & Witt, J. C. (1984). *School psychology: Essentials of theory and practice.* New York: John Wiley & Sons.

Schein, E. H. (1969). *Process consultation: Its role in organization development.* Reading, MA: Addison-Wesley.

Umansky, D. L., & Holloway, E. L. (1984). The counselor as consultant: From model to practice. *The School Counselor, 32,* 329-338.

Chapter 2

THE CONSULTANT'S ROLE

In this chapter, you will learn:

- traditional expectations for school counselors,
- alternatives to these traditional expectations,
- the importance of communication skills, and
- the importance of primary prevention.

How does a counselor's job include consultation? Administrators may not understand the basic roles and functions of the school counselor. Examples of this confusion are abundant. In a New Jersey school district, two elementary school counselors serving three schools were eliminated. Still recognizing a need for crisis counseling, the district made each school principal responsible for the counseling (Shay, 1981). This is just one example of beliefs that often make counselors the most misunderstood employees in schools.

Dissatisfaction with counselors' job performance was documented by Umansky and Holloway (1984). In their study, adults did not appreciate the counselor's role in schools. While the necessity of the teacher, custodian, and cook was understood, we believe the counselor's role is less well understood. At every grade level, counselors face challenges to their roles as counselor and consultant.

Many high school counselors have little time for counseling their students. College and vocational guidance, class scheduling, test administration, and other administrative tasks become the sole activities of a high school counselor. If any time remains, crisis counseling is often next on the list of counselor functions. The high school counselor is responsible for hundreds of students or in some schools, a thousand or more.

The elementary school counseling profession has had different but equal challenges. It did not exist thirty years ago. Limited by the perception that "little children don't have problems," no such position existed. Counselors were not a part of the elementary school.

The recent cycle of budget cuts, temporarily declining or increasing enrollments, and demand for "basics" have created an atmosphere in which the counselor's role shifts away from counseling and consultation. Although sometimes school administrators are willing to accept a limited role for the counselor as a specialist in educational, vocational, and personal counseling, this may not be the widespread assumption. The consultation role is a lesser priority, as schools reduce staff and even place counselors back into classrooms as teachers.

Umansky and Holloway commented on these traditional roles and the value of consultation.

> The counselor-as-consultant model has been lauded more recently as the way for school counselors to create a dynamic and effective profile in the schools. Consulting is considered a more efficient use of counselor services—a critical factor in light of lean school budgets. ...If counselors are to meet current and future demands for services, they should know about consultation and put it to use. (Umansky & Holloway, 1984, pp. 329-330)

COUNSELORS AS CONSULTANTS:
PERCEPTION, IDEAL, REAL

Counselors do serve as consultants. Wilgus and Shelley (1988) conducted a survey of elementary school counselors in Oregon. The pre-study on the survey identified fifteen duties elementary school counselors performed, one of which was "staff consultation—to consult with staff members regarding student academic, social or emotional progress." Other functions included parent education, parent contact, classroom programs, referrals, and staff development (areas we might consider adjuncts to consultation).

Wilgus and Shelley then asked teachers to list their perceptions of the rank order of these fifteen functions, and the ideal rank order of these functions. Finally, the school counselors were asked to keep a diary to record their actual activities.

Teachers ranked staff consultation fifth in the list of perceived functions; they ranked it fourth in the list of ideal functions: The log of actual counselor time showed consultation was third, accounting for 14% of the counselor's time. Only individual counseling (19%) and Other (15%) accounted for more counselor time (Wilgus & Shelley, 1988). This recent study clearly shows consultation is a counselor job priority.

DIFFERENCES BETWEEN HIGH SCHOOL &
ELEMENTARY SCHOOL COUNSELORS

Myrick (1977) identified specific differences between elementary and high school counselors. These distinctions are helpful to our discussion of consulting at those levels, and are as follows:

1. Historically, high school counselors preceded elementary school counselors. Their role has focused on issues such as course selection, college and vocational choices, and crisis-oriented counseling. Consultation has not been a primary responsibility.

2. Elementary school counselors are a more recent addition to schools. As child development specialists, their role has been defined by opportunities to assist teachers and parents. Consultation is a frequent role for the elementary school counselor.

We recognize the greater demand and opportunity for consultation skills in the elementary and middle high schools; therefore, many examples within this book are written to these levels. However, high school counselors have equal if unrecognized opportunities to serve as consultants. Whatever the setting, school counselors have an opportunity for consultation relationships.

A survey of state guidance supervisors by Peer (1985) provided perceptions of the secondary school counselor role and function. Over 60% felt secondary school counseling programs were not as well thought of as elementary school programs in the same district. However, the guidance directors felt most high school programs provided significant consultation services to teachers (68%), parents (51%), and administrators (65%).

A HISTORICAL REVIEW

Kahnweiler's (1979) review of the literature pertaining to the school counselor as consultant offers some clues to the present perception of the consultant's role. His review of a 21 year period (1957 to 1978) found more than 100 articles in four counseling journals. This analysis revealed a discrepancy between the quantity of articles devoted to theory and those presenting specific consultation techniques. As shown in Figure 2.1 far more articles have advocated the consultation role than practical procedures. Our observation has been that this pattern continues to exist in the research since 1978.

Recent literature is beginning to present working models of specific consultation strategies (Dinkmeyer & Carlson, 1990). We believe that the function of counselors is more than system maintenance. The consultant helps the school achieve its primary function, allowing children to achieve their human potential and build their self-esteem.

Type of Articles	Number
Models/Techniques/Guidelines	55
Basics/Trends/Opinons	35
Research/Case Study	19
Training	12
Rationale/Philosophical	10
Standards/Policies	6

Figure 2.1. Summary of articles pertaining to the school counselor as consultant, 1957 to 1978, in four counseling journals (Kahnweiler, 1979).

CONSULTATION IN ELEMENTARY SETTINGS: A REVIEW OF THE LITERATURE

Bundy and Poppen (1986) reviewed the literature pertaining to the elementary school counselor's role as consultant. Their review of relevant articles in *Elementary School Guidance and Counseling* and *The School Counselor* and cross-referenced journals was both exhaustive and rigorous. Only studies in the elementary school setting with a quantitative measurement of treatment and pretest-posttest design were included.

Twenty-one studies met the criteria for inclusion; 18 of the 21 (86%) showed significantly positive results. Seven of the 18 studies used the Adlerian approach; 6 of the 18 used a behavioral approach, and the remaining used multimodal approaches. The authors of this literature review concluded " The research studies have an important message for counselors planning consultation strategies: Consultation works" (Bundy & Poppen, 1986).

HUMAN POTENTIAL

School has an influence on each child's self-perception, or self-esteem. Research has shown that a student's self-esteem decreases as the child continues in school (Combs & Soper, 1963). Apparently, the longer you stay in school, the worse you feel about yourself! This can be anecdotally "proven" by thinking about the "average attitude" of two grade levels: first and 11th. Usually, with a decade of schooling under their belts, many high school students do not have high self-esteem. Sometimes, they no longer choose to participate in the institution, adding to the dropout rate. The school experience either builds or erodes self-esteem. In the elementary school, a child's life-style, the basic set of beliefs about self and others, is established. Often this life-style is established by the second grade.

The elementary school years profoundly affect the educational development of children. When consultants understand the interdependence of the affective (self-concept) and cognitive areas of learning, positive influences can be initiated. Our approach to this critical area is presented in two extensive educational programs (Dinkmeyer & Dinkmeyer, 1982a, 1982b). This approach is presented in Chapter 6.

CONSULTANT CHARACTERISTICS

A recent informal survey for the Association for Counselor Education and Supervision (ACES) Task Force on Consultation provides an interesting insight into perception of effective consultants. The survey asked one question: "Please list the three most important characteristics, skills or capabilities you would desire in a consultant hired to provide assistance to you on your job." The forty-nine elementary and middle school teachers responding to this question indicated six major characteristics as listed in Figure 2.2.

Many of these characteristics are consistent with our definition of effective consultation presented in Chapter 1. If consultants are effective, they must have specific knowledge and skills which they can share with the consultee.

Characteristic Desired	Number %
Knowlegeable	26
Communicative Ability/Good Listener	19
Specific Techniques/Practical Approach	11
Expertise	8
Good personality	7
Someone who has been in classroom	6

Figure 2.2. Consultant characteristics desired by elementary and middle school teachers (Dinkmeyer, Jr., 1987).

THE CONSULTANT AS A PERSON

The effective consultant possesses personal qualities and abilities which enhance effectiveness as a facilitator of human potential. The consultant's training involves course work that provides a number of required group experiences that enable the consultant to become more aware of self, impact upon others, and personal values and purposes.

The consultant is expected to be competent in the following areas:

1. *Empathy and understanding of how others feel and experience their world.*

2. *Ability to relate to children and adults in a purposeful manner.* This involves the ability to establish rapport, to develop effective working relationships, and to use time in a judicious manner. Able to establish relationships with consultees; this relationship fits consultation goals.

3. *Sensitivity to human needs.* Able to perceive a need and be available as a facilitator to help the person meet that need.

4. *Awareness of psychological dynamics, motivations, and purpose of human behavior.*

5. *Understanding of group dynamics and its significance for the educational establishment.* Aware of the impact of group forces upon the teacher, seeing the teacher in the context of forces from without (such as administration and parents) and forces from within (such as personal goals and purposes).

6. *Capability of establishing relationships that are characterized by mutual trust and mutual respect.* A consultant to either a group or an individual should inspire confidence. Mutual respect includes the belief that consultees are collaborators.

7. *Capability of taking a risk on an important issue.* Able to take a stand on significant issues that affect human development. The consultant's role requires a courageous approach to life. This involves the "courage to be imperfect," or recognizing that mistakes may be made, but realizing mistakes are learning experiences, and one is not immobilized by the fear of making mistakes. This courage is developed through group experiences and in the supervised practical experience.

8. Perhaps the most important of all, *ability to establish the necessary and sufficient conditions for a helping relationship.* The consultant should be creative, spontaneous, and imaginative. The consultant position, by its very nature, demands flexibility and the ability to deal with a variety of expectations—on one hand, the principal's need for order and structure; on the other, the child's need for participation, care, and concern.

9. *Capability of inspiring leadership at a number of levels.* Educational administrators often look to consultants as specialists in understanding human behavior, while parents see the consultant as a specialist in child psychology. Teachers see the consultant as a resource in connection with pupil personnel problems. Children might see consultants as a resource in helping them to understand self and others.

Our belief is that this type of person emerges most readily from a training program which places an emphasis upon not only the cognitive skills of the graduate student, but upon *developing an awareness of self and one's impact upon others.* We believe that this type of personal development is best arranged through regularly scheduled group experiences which enable the individual to become more aware of effect upon colleagues. The helping profession cannot tolerate the ineffectual person, the one who is able, perhaps, to relate to children but not to adults, or vice versa. The school consultant must be capable of establishing human relationships.

These are high standards. Not all consultants will attain this level upon completion of training, and personal growth is a continual process. However, we need to recognize these traits are not mere platitudes. Course work alone does not develop adequate consultants. **No single factor is more destructive to consultant progress than lack of ability to develop effective helping relationships.**

COMMUNICATION IN CONSULTATION

The consultant is not only a specialist in human relationships but also in communication. Messages sent by both consultants and consultees are always multifaceted, including content and feeling. As an active and skilled listener, **the consultant must hear both the words and the feelings in order to get the message from the consultee.** The consultant helps the client to become a more effective listener by hearing the total message.

Some messages are incongruent. The consultant should look for words which may be different from the feeling. For example, a variety of ways exists for saying "I am happy" or "I am angry" to make feelings incongruent with the words. One must note tone of voice, facial expression, and other nonverbal clues. The consultant is aware of various methods of dealing with stress. Virginia Satir (1967) developed a classic format for analyzing the difference between manipulative and actualization response forms. The consultant's goal is to develop responses where the communication is characterized by hearing, listening, understanding, and mutual meaning. The types of responses include the following:

1. **Placating**—This style of response is used by a person who always keeps safe, attempts to placate, or be the martyr. The person crosses self out as unimportant and is willing to agree with anything the other person offers.

2. **Blaming**—This style of response is used by the person who is aggressive. This person is suspicious others take advantage and essentially believes "Only I am important." Others don't count, so they are crossed out. This has been classified as "the boss" response.

3. **Conniving and Reasonable**—This style of response is used by communicators who put an emphasis on being correct and in not letting any know their weaknesses. They speak as if they were computers and have no feelings.

4. **Avoiding and Irrelevant**—This style of response is used by the person who essentially talks as if he/she has no relationship to others, almost as if he/she were "psychotic." This person says, "I am not here and you are not here." No attempt is made to communicate.

5. **Congruent**—This style of response equals real communication in which the affect and words are congruent. A person who makes a congruent response creates a relationship which is real and safe. The consultant models this level of responding as consultees and clients work toward it. (Satir, 1967)

Although many systems to evaluate the quality of communication have been developed since Satir's work, the underlying assumptions remain consistent. A **low-level response** does not acknowledge content. A **medium-level response** begins to understand the feeling within the statement. **The highest level response** understands both content and feeling in a way that adds to the dialogue.

Although Satir is often cited as a classic example of a helpful communications approach, other mental health professionals continue to expand this area. Hawes (1989) presented a method of communication training between teachers and children in which the school counselor was a consultant and trainer. The reader is referred to it as a concrete and comprehensive approach to communication training which is consistent with our approach.

Verbal messages too often are destructive and do not facilitate growth. Communication is at times ineffective because we send ineffectual messages. Examples of these ineffective messages include procedures such as the following:

1. **Ordering and commanding** are ineffective because they deny the mutual aspect of the consultation relationship.

2. **Warning and admonishing** consultees to stop certain behaviors reflects an attitude that communicates judgment. Guilt or resentment will follow.

3. **Exhorting and moralizing** present messages such as "My way is best." They deny the right of the consultee to make decisions.

4. **Advising and providing solutions** without hearing the consultee's situation derails the consultation relationship.

5. **Lecturing** is best left for university courses. It is an ineffective consultation style.

6. **Judging and criticizing** elevates the role of the consultant so that consultant and consultee are no longer on an equal communication level.

7. **Praising and agreeing** are ineffective motivation techniques.

8. **Name calling and ridiculing** are best left for the playground.

9. **Interpreting and analyzing** should not be the beginning states of a consultation relationship.

10. **Reassuring and sympathizing** may be perceived as false. They are not effective encouragement skills.

11. **Probing, questioning, and interrogating** may be inappropriate if the consultee is not ready.

12. **Withdrawing, humoring, and diverting** do not accurately reflect consultee's situation.

Many consultee statements may bring about ineffective communication. The consultant develops congruent communications and is alert to any ineffectual communication with the consultee. **Helping the consultee to become aware of** *ineffective communication patterns is an important step in the consultation relationship.*

CONSULTANT LEADS AND VERBAL TRANSACTIONS

Consultation can be limited in its effectiveness. Verbal and nonverbal messages may restrict open communication. A consultant's limited conception of the role may create the perception of an "expert," able to answer all questions. If the staff accepts the image, they present their problems.

Instead, the process must be collaborative with total involvement of the consultee for the productive hypotheses to be generated and workable corrective procedures to be established. The parable of either fishing for a person or teaching them to fish illustrates our point. The former requires daily interaction; the latter, one lesson.

Effective consulting is tailored to the uniqueness of both the client and the consultee. This establishes communication that is open. It deals with all of the messages, especially the feelings and personal meanings in the content which are often not understood in ordinary social conversations or communications between professionals.

These procedures must go beyond telling, lecturing, advising, and sharing "pedagogics." In contrast, one must establish an atmosphere which encourages sharing and exploring ideas. *Effective consulting engages the cognitive and affective domains.* It seeks to examine and share ideas, openly exploring the feelings of all concerned, and to move toward commitments to action. The relationship operates on the premise that emotional communication is two-way, insofar as it elicits feedback and processes the feedback continuously to clarify the messages that are being sent and their meanings.

The essence of consultation is communication. The consultant must be able to understand those messages being sent and be sensitive to the relationship with the consultee. This necessitates being aware of one's verbal and nonverbal communication and the impressions that are being developed in the transactions with the staff.

A consultant lead is the initiation of a transaction or the response to the consultee. **Consultant leads** influence the responses of the consultee and may focus on four different kinds of techniques.

1. *Techniques that focus on content*

   - Encouraging continuation, such as "Tell me about..."
   - Verifying beliefs, such as "You seem to believe..."
   - Asking questions that systematically explore the transactions with the client such as

     What did you do?

     What did the child do?

     How did the child respond?

     How did you respond?

     How did you feel?

     What did you do about the child's response?

     What was the child's reaction to your response?

2. *Techniques that elicit affect and encourage feeling.* These facilitate the consultee becoming aware of personal feelings and enable the consultant to express understanding, feelings, and empathy. Eliciting affect gets the whole person involved in the consultation.

   - Restatement of feeling

- Reflection of feeling
- Silence

3. ***Techniques designed to facilitate self-understanding and awareness of one's own part in the transactions.***

   - Clarification, such as "You believe..."
   - Restatement of content
   - Restatement of content and its hidden message
   - Questions which enable the consultee to see the psychological movement in transactions with the client.

4. ***Techniques designed to facilitate new responses.*** Procedures for improving the consultee-client relationship, and methods of modifying behavior:

   - Encouragement
   - Development of choices
   - Enlargement of consultee's view and presentation of alternatives
   - Establish goals
   - Establish procedures
   - Formulate change strategies

These leads must be accomplished with appropriate timing and sensitivity to the consultee. Techniques must account for the consultee's personality and willingness to change.

Leads are a function of the personality and theoretical bias of the consultant. They cannot be used mechanically. For example, development of choices is only effective when used in a climate where threat and fear are minimized and the relationship is not perceived to be judgmental. The evaluation and diagnosis are always done in collaboration with the consultee. The consultant cannot prescribe for the consultee. Prescriptions or diagnosis without feedback and acceptance are ineffective. The written reports filed in most large pupil personnel psychologists' and administrators' files are testimony to the intellectual exercise performed in this one-way communication.

CONSULTATION PROCESSES

Comparing effective to ineffective consultant/consultee communication patterns, in effective, goals are mutually aligned, and the consultee participates in terms of perceptions, beliefs, values, and attitudes that influence assumptions about students and the education process. When the consultee begins, the consultant listens closely. These opening statements influence the relationship. The probability of a collaborative diagnosis and treatment is being established. Early transactions are crucial. They must create a climate, establish communication, and set a pattern for ensuing contacts. At the same time, early transactions must provide some help to the consultee with the current concern.

Consultants may err in terms of being highly directive, developing ready answers or instant **pat solutions**. "Give her more love," "Individualize the instruction," and "Reinforce his good behavior" are quick replies. None of these "solutions" are necessarily bad, but they must be designed to fit the assets and liabilities involved in the transactions between consultant and consultee. Pat answers may cause the consultee to consider the consultant's ideas as superficial.

The more **active leads**, such as **disclosure, confrontation,** and **tentative hypotheses**, may provoke resistance. When the consultant is involved in sharing perceptions that come from an external frame of reference, these perceptions may be perceived as judgments or authoritarian statements. Resistance against a collaborative relationship may be the result. However, active leads do not necessarily inhibit the consultation process if they are aligned with the consultee's personal meaning and subjective perceptions.

Confrontation can serve as a vehicle to bring the client in direct touch with personal experience. Honest confrontation can elicit constructive therapeutic process, movement, and ultimately constructive gain or change. Confrontation can help the consultee to become aware of the lack of harmony among goals, philosophy, and actions or practices.

The **diagnosis** is facilitated by the collaborative exploration of the current life situation, the perceptions of both client and consultee, and the open and honest feedback about any and all impressions which are generated. This phase is unique in its emphasis on searching for assets and strengths in the consultee and the client. The consultant must recognize that while the less active leads have less potential for harm, they also have greater potential for being circular, impotent, and unable to move the consultee towards awareness and new procedures.

SOCIETY AND SCHOOLS

Adults are products of societal educational institutions. Our classroom, school, and consulting relationships do not have to be autocratic and inhumane. We are suggesting that we can strive for nothing less than an enlightened and compassionate school. This clearly recognizes that we do not produce compassionate, humane people by focusing only on cognition and intellectual gain. If we are to exist together as equals, humaneness must become a stated rather than implied goal of the educational process.

Feelings of Adequacy and Failure

An increasing number of children and adolescents do not succeed in the educational process as it is presently organized. The evidence is apparent when one looks at problems related to underachievement, drug and alcohol abuse, dropouts, and the apathy of some students who remain within the system. Our society is regularly producing a large number of children and adults who perceive themselves as inadequate and as failures.

William Glasser, a psychiatrist interested in education, drew some generalizations related to failure and discovered the following principle: "Regardless of how many failures a person has had in his past, regardless of his background, his culture, his color, or his economic level, he will not succeed in general until he can in some way first experience success in one important part of his life" (Glasser, 1969, p.5). Glasser's contention was that if the child is able to succeed in school, that child will have an excellent chance for success in life. In contrast, failure in the school diminishes the chance to be a success in life.

Schools are a product of a failure-oriented evaluation system and a mistake-centered approach to instruction. Schools are more concerned with children's weaknesses and liabilities than with their strengths and assets. However, if schools are to meet the problems of the "rebel," the "unmotivated," the "apathetic," the "alienated," and the general social disorganization that surrounds us, they must start to examine the deficiencies which appear in parts of the educational system.

Our current emphasis on standards, threats, and punishment prevents the development of a feeling of genuine self-worth. Schools have failed to teach children how to maintain a successful identity and to become socially responsible, contributing persons. Children come to school feeling capable and comparatively adequate, but the school quickly creates feelings of inadequacy.

Perhaps our emphasis should have been on persons who are truly committed to the learning process instead of memorization. In contrast, schools focus on memorization and failure and little on problem solving, spontaneity, creativity, involvement, interest, and the capacity to think. In our overemphasis upon a mistake-centered type of education which places emphasis upon the one right answer, we have failed to develop citizens who care, are concerned and who are committed to action. Educated citizens in a democracy learn how to become effective human beings by participating in decision-making processes related to their own educations. We learn how to decide by being given choices. We become responsible by accepting responsibility for the consequences of decisions, attitudes, and behavior.

STAGES OF THE CONSULTATION PROCESS

The consultation process can be broken into stages. General agreement does not exist as to what these stages are. Brown, Kurpius, and Morris (1988) suggested five or six steps but also pointed out several established models which ignore some of these steps. For example, many consultation models stress the importance of building a relationship, while others ignore it.

Several common characteristics of the process can be identified. First, the process can be seen as problem-solving. Second, any definition of stages or steps must not use them as independent, discrete stages. The consultation may return to an earlier stage or jump ahead to a later stage. Finally, parallel processes between the consultant and consultee, and the consultee and client must be recognized. Both relationships have stages.

Stages are neither arbitrary nor absolute. They reflect our understanding of the consultation process. Five stages are discussed: establish the relationship, gather data and identify the problem, set goals, use strategies, and evaluation. The first stage is discussed in this chapter, with subsequent chapters dealing with the remaining stages.

Establish the Relationship

Most previous literature on consultation stresses the importance of establishing the relationship. Few have addressed the complex nature of the school consultant's role. This role may depend on whether or not the consultant is based within the building in which the consultation occurs.

If the consultant is not based in the particular school, one is perceived as an outsider. Many schools consist of twenty or more adult faculty and staff. They can become a tightly-knit social system with norms and expectations. The norm "How do we feel about outside advice?" is worth examining.

Detecting this attitude may occur while developing the relationship. If the consultee has directly requested the consultation, the consultant is more likely to be accepted, at least initially. Acceptance may even be a topic for discussion while establishing the relationship.

If the consultant is based *inside* that school, the task may be no easier. Consultees must view the consultant in a new light. A school teacher and a school counselor may be capable of establishing a new relationship, but to do so will require direction from the consultant.

Skills in this stage of the relationship can be drawn from previous counselor training. **Listening** and **attending** are important. **Body language**, **eye contact**, and **reflective listening** are all part of the consultant's abilities at this stage.

Other Issues While Establishing the Relationship. The beginning of the relationship poses specific concerns for the consultant. **Confidentiality** is essential but often overlooked.

The ground rules must be established so that both parties understand the limits. This issue is inherent in consultation; *a third party is involved*. The consultant must be careful to not promise total confidentiality. The issue, instead, should be resolved in a process of mutual agreement. Confidentiality is essential, yet complex. A full discussion of this issue is found in Brown et al. (1988). We also urge full knowledge of your state laws concerning counselor-client confidentiality. At least twenty states now have rules concerning this relationship.

An example of the complexity of this issue follows. A teacher involves the counselor as a consultant regarding a child in the classroom. During the process of gathering data the consultant believes that the child's school problems may be due in part to abuse and neglect in the home. The consultant (or any adult) is bound by state law to report any suspected child abuse. However, the teacher does not believe abuse is occurring and terminates the consultation relationship. What does the consultant do?

This example highlights the real risks and challenges in the consultation relationship. Whether an external or internal consultant, establishing the relationship includes a mutually agreed boundary for confidentiality.

Another issue at the beginning of a consultation relationship is *equality*. Consultation relationships strive for equality between the participants. Consultees often do not perceive their role as equal; they have a problem and are seeking answers. They see their part in the relationship as inferior.

This perceived less-than position makes the consultant's encouragement skills essential. Consultants can stress equality by directly stating this belief, or can imply the same through a variety of behaviors. Equality behaviors focus on recognizing assets and efforts, responsibility for the consultee, and encouragement through listening, structuring, and decision-making collaboration.

The third area of concern at the start of a consultation relationship concerns the **crossover** between counseling and consultation. The recommendation is that consultants do not become counselors within the same relationship. This creates a dual relationship.

The recommendation is a difficult rule to follow, especially when one is trained as a counselor. **The consultation relationship must focus on the third party**, not the consultee. In theory, consultation and counseling are mutually exclusive.

What if a consultee presents a personal situation that lends itself to counseling? The consultant must realize the dangers on crossing over the line into counseling.

A consultant was asked to work with a seventh grade teacher, Mrs. M. She presented challenges with two students and stated, "They make me so mad. They remind me of my kids." Here the consultant could take the focus from the two students into Mrs. M's children, turning the relationship into counseling. The consultation would shift and the focus would be lost.

The consultant would use listening skills to establish credibility with the consultee. Should that listening include issues related to the consultee's personal life, it is not consultation. The consultant must either reframe the relationship, make a referral, or terminate the relationship.

The fourth concern at the beginning of consultation relationships is the necessity for **communication skills** by the consultant. Various texts do justice to this core counselor competency. To outline the necessary communication skills is not within the scope of this book. However, consultation cannot occur without communications competency.

Another issue relates to **cultural differences**. Differences between cultures exist and affect a consultant's ability to work effectively within the consultee's culture. Two examples demonstrate this situation:

I was asked to consult with parents in a school district composed primarily of Mexican Americans in the United States southwest. Some of my information portrayed fathers playing an active role in home chores. This, I was told, was not the role fathers play in many families.

Presenting similar materials in the Japanese culture presented challenges in the area of adolescent and child responsibilities. While a general agreement prevailed that children should have responsibility, little interest in allowing a child to experience consequences of choices such as not doing homework was expressed. Parents said, "The stakes are too high. They can think for themselves once they have a good job."

Both incidents illustrate the consultant's cultural beliefs contrasting with differing consultee cultural beliefs. This contrast raises an interesting question as to which view is "right."

Specific African-American and White cultural concerns were raised by Gibbs (1980). The differences focus on the initial orientations to consultation. According to Gibbs, African-Americans prejudge interpersonal competency and Whites prejudge technical competency before committing to a consultation relationship. No proof of this theory is presented, but it highlights differences to which consultants must be sensitive. Although we are becoming more homogenized, be aware of differences which relate to culture.

Establishing the consultation relationship includes basic communication skills, confidentiality issues, and sensitivity to cultural issues. It also delineates the differences between consultation and counseling, and maintains a difference between the two types of relationships.

SUMMARY

The consultant's role has been heavily researched and delineated throughout the literature for more than twenty years. We have highlighted major issues, including the nature of the relationship, its effectiveness, and steps in the consultation process. In the remainder of this book, we set forth our theory and practice of consultation.

REVIEW QUESTIONS

1. How are school counselors perceived by other school professionals?

2. What are the differences between elementary and high school counselors? How do you account for these differences, and what do they imply for a consultation relationship?

3. What do teachers see as desirable characteristics from consultants?

4. What are ineffective communication styles from consultants? Give examples whenever possible.

5. What are effective communication styles from consultants? Again, give examples.

6. Discuss both the unique and common characteristics of the stages of the consultation process.

REFERENCES

Brown, D., Kurpius, D.J., & Morris, J.R. (1988). *Handbook of consultation with individuals and small groups.* Alexandria, VA: Association for Counselor Education and Supervision.

Bundy, M.L, & Poppen, W.A. (1986). School counselors' effectiveness as consultants: A research review. *Elementary School Guidance and Counseling, 20,* 215-222.

Combs, A., & Soper, D. (1963). *The relationship of child perceptions to adjustment and behavior in early school years.* Washington, DC: Cooperative Research Project, Office of Health, Education and Welfare.

Dinkmeyer, D., & Dinkmeyer, D., Jr. (1982a). *Developing understanding of self and others: DUSO 1.* Circle Pines, MN: American Guidance Service.

Dinkmeyer, D., & Dinkmeyer, D., Jr. (1982b). *Developing understanding of self and others: DUSO 2.* Circle Pines, MN: American Guidance Service.

Dinkmeyer, D., Jr. (1987). Consultation competency preferences from school teachers. Unpublished research.

Dinkmeyer, D., Jr., & Carlson, J. (1990). Guidance in a small school. *The School Counselor, 37,* 199-203.

Gibbs, J.T. (1980). The interpersonal orientation in mental health consultation: Toward a model of ethnic variations in consultation. *Journal of Community Psychology. 8,* 195-207.

Glasser, W. (1969). *Schools without failure.* New York: Harper and Row.

Hawes, D. (1989). Communication between teachers and children: A counselor consultant/trainer model. *Elementary School Guidance and Counseling, 24,* 58-67.

Kahnweiler, W.M. (1979). The school counselor as consultant: A historical review. *Personnel and Guidance Journal,* 4/79, 374-380.

Myrick, R.D. (1977). *Consultation as a counselor intervention.* Ann Arbor, MI: ERIC Counseling and Personnel Services Clearinghouse.

Peer, G.G. (1985). The status of secondary school guidance: A national survey. *The School Counselor,* 32(3), 181-189.

Satir, V. (1967). *Conjoint family therapy* (rev. ed). Palo Alto, CA: Science and Behavior Books.

Shay, M. (1981). Are today's economics crunching counselor services? *NASSP Bulletin,* 65, 10-16.

Umansky, D.L., & Holloway, E.L. (1984). The counselor as consultant: From model to practice. *The School Counselor,* 31(4), 329-338.

Wilgus, E., & Shelley, V. (1988). The role of the elementary-school counselor: Teacher perceptions, expectations, and actual function. *The School Counselor,* 35(3), 259-266.

Chapter 3

A CONSULTATION THEORY

In this chapter, you will learn:

- unhelpful consultant beliefs;
- a rationale for the Adlerian approach;
- effective consultant beliefs;
- nine rules of behavior, including goals of misbehavior; and
- discipline strategies.

Every consultant has a personal understanding of human behavior. This understanding is, in fact, a theory of human behavior. Your theory may be based on life experiences, reading in books, course work in graduate school, and in-service workshops. If we add to this a systematic, accurate set of beliefs, we have clues toward changing behaviors.

Theory for theory's sake has value only to the intellectual. *The consultant requires a theory that is practical and proficient*. Such an approach to understanding human behavior is frequently lacking in consultation. Teachers, in their efforts to eliminate undesirable behaviors, may adopt a set of rules or regulations which appear to solve the problem. Pat answers, advice, and quick solutions have no underlying understanding of behavior, misbehavior, and motivation.

In this chapter, we present a theory of consultation based in Adlerian psychology. Founded by Alfred Adler and developed across North America by Rudolf Dreikurs, Adlerian Psychology is well suited to the needs of the consultant. It offers ideas on misbehavior, discipline, motivation, and relationships. The psychology is appropriate for educators as well as those with more psychological backgrounds.

INEFFECTIVE BELIEFS

Many popular beliefs about the cause of human behavior are ineffective. The **external frame of reference** is an example of such an approach. It is illustrated in the following example.

A student has high test scores but does not do well in school. This is contradictory information—the test scores show ability, and yet, the student is not performing. What is the explanation? The external frame of reference looks to causes outside the student for explanation. These causes might be a poor environment or home situation, poor relationships with peers or teachers, or any other reasons outside the student.

Externally-based explanations for behavior and misbehavior include the following:

Sex-role stereotype—Although less prevalent today as compared to twenty years ago, teachers and parents may excuse male assertive misbehavior and female inadequacy behaviors simply because of gender. The phrase "boys will be boys" expresses such a lack of understanding. Stereotyping by gender can include athletic or intellectual ability or inability. It also encompasses behavior expectations: boys are uncooperative, girls are compliant.

Heredity—Our present understanding of genetics does not allow us to conclude it is a primary cause of behavior and misbehavior. Research in this area would suggest tendencies and patterns, but it is not sufficient as a separate explanation for personality.

Environment—Where the student lives, the socioeconomic status of the family, and single, dual, or stepparent family structures are not primary causes of behavior and misbehavior.

Ages and stages—Behavior is due to a particular age, such as the "terrible twos" or the challenging teenage years.

Increasingly turbulent and negative external factors are surrounding today's students. Divorce, drugs, job transfers, and other stressors make it difficult to remember the "Father Knows Best" years of our culture. In the final analysis, however, these external factors are usually not the sole or predominant cause of a student's personality. Consultants have few, if any, effective recommendations or strategies if these external factors are the sole cause of the problem.

The external frame of reference also looks for many facts and opinions. Case studies or staffings bring together many points of view. The emphasis is on opinions, preferably representing a unbiased scientific approach.

For example, when a case study or an individual analysis is conducted, specialists from various disciplines (e.g., music, social work, administration, physical education, psychology) bring in facts and details as to how the student performs. Each brings a piece of the puzzling student. These pieces of the puzzle do not necessarily result in a coherent picture. The points made by each profession do not necessarily result in an accurate picture of the child's personality or decisions. Each may be "true," as seen by that adult, but the collective opinion may not present the child in the most helpful perspective.

Behavior is better understood through the **internal frame of reference**. How does the behavior "make sense" to that student? Because behavior is a function of an individual's perceptions, understand the student's (or consultee's) perceptions. Careful observation can identify the feelings, attitudes, and purposes of the student.

Understanding behavior in simple, helpful terms is the Adlerian approach. Sometimes this is called Individual Psychology. Many prior written works have been prepared for parents, teachers, and counselors based on Adlerian Psychology (Dinkmeyer, McKay, & Dinkmeyer, 1980; Dinkmeyer, Dinkmeyer, & Sperry,1987; Dinkmeyer & McKay, 1989; Painter & Corsini, 1990; Cater, 1992).

RATIONALE FOR THE ADLERIAN APPROACH TO CONSULTATION

The purpose of the consultation process is to increase the human potential of the teacher, administrator, student, and parent. Each individual has a considerable creative capacity to understand, to change, and to learn. When we begin a consultation relationship, we seek to tap this creative capacity in the consultee. In turn, the skills we teach the consultee have an impact on those whom the consultee influences.

For example, Ms. Jones may enter into a consulting relationship with a school counselor. She might want to change the behavior of several students in her classroom. She believes the students are not functioning at their potential. The teacher is seeking change, and comes to the consultant for that change. Thus we find the basis for a beginning in the consultation relationship, a desire for change.

The recognition that a "problem" exists is a basis for the relationship between consultant and consultee. In Chapter 1, we identified three parts to the consulting relationship: consultant, consultee, and "problem/person." Effective consulting relationships separate the problem from the person.

For example, a teacher comes to the consultant with a "problem student." Is the consultation problem (1) the student, (2) the student's beliefs which fuel the undesirable behaviors, (3) the teacher's beliefs about the student and student behaviors, or (4) the teacher's lack of effective behaviors to deal with the student? The four possibilities may confuse the basic "problem" in the consultation.

In the Adlerian approach, **beliefs** are examined in addition to behaviors. We collect data on behaviors which allow us to understand the inherent beliefs. In the above case of the "problem student," we listen to descriptions of behaviors in order to get a better picture of the teacher and student beliefs which generate these behaviors.

EFFECTIVE CONSULTANT BELIEFS

Your behavior is influenced by your belief system. Effective consultants have beliefs about people which are different from ineffective consultants.

For example, are all people capable? Refusal to allow others to function (by taking on all responsibility) would be inconsistent with that belief. Another example is recommending better listening skills, but exhibiting poor listening in a conversation with the teacher:

Teacher: *They sure make me angry!*

Consultant: *I suggest you give them more love.*

Teacher: *I'll try! But they really make me angry.*

Consultant: *It's also important to listen and hear their feelings.*

Teacher: *Yes, but they still make me mad!*

The consultant failed to hear the teacher's feeling, or to realize that the proposed suggestion was not congruent with the teacher's problem. The consultant believed to listen and hear feelings was important but did not hear the anger in the teacher's statement.

A more effective dialogue would include the consultant hearing the immediate feelings of the teacher:

Teacher: *They sure make me angry!*

Consultant: *You're angry about your students.*

Teacher: *Yes, they just don't listen. Some seem to want to make me mad.*

The consultant deals directly with the teacher's anger. It leads to clues as to what beliefs the students have when angering the teacher.

An effective approach also allows for erroneous judgments and has the ability to modify a faulty tentative hypothesis.

Here the consultant misjudges the intensity of the teacher's feelings:

Teacher: *They make me angry!*

Consultant: *You're absolutely furious at your students.*

Teacher: *No, I don't let them get to me. I'd be crazy by now.*

Consultant: *But there are times when they do things that make you angry.*

Teacher: *Yes.*

The consultant misjudged the intensity of feelings. Rather than convince the teacher that the assessment was correct, the consultant corrects and tries again. The second effort is confirmed by the consultee.

Even if the teacher does get furious at the students (the consultant may know this from the principal, parents, or other observers), a more helpful place to begin is with the consultee's own perceptions.

In consultation, do we focus on the student, the teacher, or both? In counseling, the counselor helps people to understand themselves, and to modify their behaviors. **In consulting, the consultant helps the consultee to directly understand self, others, the relationship between self and others, and procedures to modify behavior.**

Most conventional definitions of consultation emphasize the differences between counseling and consulting as shown in Figure 3.1. We use the example of a counselor, teacher, and student to illustrate these differences.

In Figure 3.1, the emphasis is on "primary" and "secondary" relationships. Counselors, in both cases, meet with teachers but the difference is upon the emphasis. In consultation, the emphasis is upon the student.

Consulting	Counseling
Roles	
Counselor = Consultant	Counselor = Counselor
Teacher = Consultee	Teacher = Teacher
Student = "3rd party"	Student = Student
Secondary Relationship	
Consultant <—> Consultee	Teacher <—> Student
Consultant <—> 3rd party	
Primary Relationship	
Consultee <—> 3rd party	Teacher <—> Student
Consultant <—> 3rd party	

Figure 3.1. Differences between consultation and counseling.

A practical consultation theory includes:

- an understanding of human behavior,

- a procedure that helps the consultant to accurately communicate this understanding to others, and

- operational knowledge of how to implement or put this understanding into practice.

Eliminating undesirable behavior in the classroom is challenging. Many times suggestions will reinforce it and cause it to occur more frequently, thereby making it harder to change. The following example illustrates the unintentional, uninformed approach. Notice how the teacher reinforces the behavior she wants to eliminate:

Ms. Roeder, a fifth-grade teacher, wanted to keep Marianne in her seat during class. Whenever Marianne would get out of her chair, Ms. Roeder would yell at her, *"Get in that seat!"*

and she would quickly comply. After talking to the consultant, Ms. Roeder decided to ignore Marianne's behavior in hopes that it would go away. After two days, she reported to the consultant, *"It's no use. When I ignore her, she gets worse! She pulls the hair of other students, drops books—she just doesn't stay in her chair. I give up!"*

Many teachers are troubled by this and similar dilemmas. Behavior often gets worse before it gets better. The teacher must force herself to ignore misbehavior. Ms. Roeder may have been able to deal with the situation more effectively. The result at this time, however, was that Marianne's attention-getting behavior was strengthened rather than weakened, and her goal moved to power in an effort to control the classroom.

NINE IDEAS ABOUT BEHAVIOR

The following ideas are part of the Adlerian approach to consulting. Notice how the beliefs of the consultant and the consultee are critical to changing behaviors. In our experience, many of the following nine ideas have never been known to consultees. Therefore, the consultation relationship can have a strong educational emphasis.

1. Human Personality Is Understood by Its Unity or Pattern, the Life-style.

Why did Marianne want to gain attention in Ms. Roeder's classroom? Isolated incidents or causal explanations such as peer influences or poor home environment can be explanations. However, a more useful procedure is to look at Marianne in the total context of her behavior.

Instead of analyzing elements of a person's personality, look at the pattern. Historically, school personnel have looked at the student as a collection of pieces—test score, IQ scores, past grades, and teacher comments. When these are viewed individually, they have little meaning. Effective consultants look for the pattern to the pieces. This pattern is the personality.

Does an early elementary school student have a definable personality? We believe that personality is defined by the time a child is five or six years old. This definable personality is called the life-style. The life-style also can be seen as a characteristic pattern of beliefs and choices. For example, *"I am a troublemaker"* or *"I can help people"* are beliefs which contribute to a life-style.

If your prior training is not counseling, you may have been exposed to different theories and ideas about personality development (although counseling itself has many ideas about personality, too). For example, the nurse approaches the individual from a physiological standpoint, the social worker from a social relationship approach, and the psychologist from a psychological standpoint. Each profession understands a particular element.

A person is more than health, social relationships, or mental abilities. The total being has thoughts, feelings, and beliefs working in concert to maintain the life-style. We must understand the pattern and help the person in relation to this pattern or life-style.

The unity or pattern of a student's behavior is therefore often misunderstood. Equally important, the consultant can misunderstand the pattern of a consultee's behaviors if the broadest possible picture is not examined. The often-told story of the blind men at the elephant has been told to illustrate this point. To one man, elephants were thick and stout (the leg); to another long and thin (the tail), and to another very sharp (the tusk). The pieces were very different and contradictory. Together, they give a true picture of the elephant.

Labels and categories for students contribute to a fragmentary analysis of behaviors. Students are considered "underachievers," "scholars," or other common descriptors. How could a scholar get in trouble after school, and how could an underachiever do so well on that test (they must have been cheating)? Labels create misleading and useless conclusions. The unity and pattern of any person, including very young students, is expressed in the life-style.

2. Behavior Is Goal Directed and Purposeful.

The Adlerian approach stresses the purposeful nature of behavior. All behavior has a goal or purpose. This goal may not be known to the behaver (or student) but this does not prevent the person from seeking the goal. The goal-directness of behavior applies to misbehavior as well as positive behavior.

The concept of goal-directness is an essential, important concept for the consultant. It opens new perceptions on seemingly confusing behaviors. In many ways, goals of behavior are both an assessment and an answer to many consultee's questions. Goals are clues to a person's intentions (the assessment) and what can be done about it (the answer).

Consultation with teachers and parents often concerns misbehaviors. Understanding the misbehavior purposefully helps both the consultant and consultee. It also allows the consultee to understand how corrective actions might be taken.

Bruce has become a problem for his teacher. He does not do his homework, and is frequently argumentative in the classroom. When the teacher asks Bruce why he hasn't done his homework, he replies, *"I don't want to do it, and you can't make me."* The teacher replies, *"You can't say that to me, young man. If you don't do your homework, I'm going to call your parents."* As the teacher walks away, Bruce has a sly smile on his face.

The purpose of Bruce's misbehavior is power. He is engaged in a power struggle with his teacher, attempting to prove who is in control. When the teacher brings more power into the conflict (by threatening to contact the parents), Bruce is pleased at this powerful response. He knows that his parents may not be concerned with his schoolwork. This attempt by the teacher to defeat his powerful resistance will not work.

In most consultations the goals of misbehavior are essential parts of the consultation relationship. Goal-directed behavior helps to diagnose problems about the third party. It gives a frame of reference for both consultant and consultee to work with the problem.

Two final concepts must be addressed in the context of behavior. Each person behaves according to his or her own **private logic**; the unwritten set of rules which constitute the life-style. The **creative capacity** to choose is also at work in life-style development.

Four Goals of Misbehavior. Rudolf Dreikurs found that misbehavior in children occurred in one of four goals: **attention**, **power**, **revenge**, and to **display inadequacy.** When asked how he came to these conclusions, Dreikurs is reported to have said, *"I did not invent these goals, I merely observed them."*

Dreikurs and others have discussed goals of misbehavior in numerous articles, books, and workshops. One of these discussions is in Dinkmeyer and McKay's *The Parent's Handbook* (1989). Although that context is parent and child, the student and teacher and consultant/consultee relationships are applicable.

Because all people are social, decision making beings, our decisions about behavior are based on the decision about **how to belong**, to find a place of significance. If this belonging can be done positively, fine. If belonging is achieved through negative behavior (in the behaver's perception), fine, too. Misbehavior comes from a perception, or belief of discouragement.

We can look at misbehavior from three perspectives: the belief behind the behavior, the behavior itself, or the payoff (goal or consequence) of the behavior. The most helpful procedure is to first look at the goal or consequence of the behavior.

In Figure 3.2, "The Goals of Misbehavior" are illustrated. **Goals, beliefs, feelings, and alternatives** are outlined in this figure. To learn how to identify a specific goal, use this two-step method:

(1). What is your reaction to the child's misbehavior? What do you feel, and do, when the child misbehaves?

(2). What does the child do in response to your behaviors?

In examination of Figure 3.2, one will find differences between the four goals in terms of feelings and reactions. Goals appear to increase in intensity from attention to power and revenge, whereas the fourth goal seems less intense. The explanation for this progression is increasing discouragement about belonging in the classroom or other group in a positive way.

Seven Goals of Teen Misbehavior. The four goals of misbehavior have been expanded when looking at the misbehavior of teens. Dinkmeyer and McKay (1990) have presented seven goals of teen misbehavior. The three additional goals of **excitement, peer acceptance,** and **superiority** are reflections of the teens' interest in moving *away* from the adult-defined groups into their own groups. These ideas are discussed in Figure 3.3.

(Continued on page 70)

The Goals of Misbehavior

Child's Faulty Belief	Child's Goal*	Parent's Feeling and Reaction	Child's Response to Parent's Attempts at Correction	Alternatives for Parents
I belong *only* when I am being noticed or served.	Attention	Feeling: Annoyed Reaction: Tendency to remind and coax.	Temporarily stops misbehavior. Later resumes same behavior or dusturbs in another way.	Ignore misbehavior when possible. Give attention for positive behavior when child is not making a bid for it. Avoid undue service. Realize that reminding, punishing, rewarding, coaxing, and service are undue attention.
I belong *only* when I am in control or am boss, or when I am proving no one can boss me!	Power	Feeling: Angry, provoked, as if one's authority is threatened Reaction: Tendency to fight or to give in.	Active- or passive-aggressive misbehavior is intensified, or child submits with "defiant compliance."	Withdraw from conflict. Help child see how to use power constructively by appealing for child's help and enlisting cooperation. Realize that fighting or giving in only increases child's desire for power.
I belong *only* by hurting others as I feel hurt. I cannot be loved.	Revenge	Feeling: Deeply hurt Reaction: Tendency to retaliate and get even	Seeks further revenge by intensifying misbehavior or choosing another weapon.	Avoid feeling hurt. Avoid punishment and retaliation. Build trusting relationship; convince child that she is loved.

| I belong *only* by convincing others not to expect anything from me. I am unable; I am helpless. | **Display of Inadequacy** | Feeling: Despair; hopelessness; "I give up" Reaction: Tendency to agree with child that nothing can be done | Passively responds or fails to respond to whatever is done. Shows no improvement. | Stop all criticism. Encourage any positive attempt, no matter how small; focus on assets. Above all, don't be hooked into pity, and don't give up. |

*To determine your child's goal, you must check your feelings and the child's response to your attempts to correct him or her.

Goal identification is simplified by observing:

  a. Your own feelings and reaction to the child's misbehavior.

  b. The child's response to your attempts at correction.

By considering your situation in terms of the chart, you will be able to identify the goal of the misbehavior.

Figure 3.2. The four goals of misbehavior. Source: *Systematic Training for Effective Parenting* (STEP): *The Parent's Handbook* by Dinkmeyer and McKay, 1989 (3rd Edition), American Guidance Service, Inc. Circle Pines MN 55014-1796. Reproduced with permission.

The Goals of Teen Misbehavior
The basic Four Goals

Teen's Faulty Belief	Goal	Example*	Parent's Feelings and reactions	Teen's Response to Parent's Reaction
I belong only when:				
I am being noticed or served.	**Attention**	Active: Clowning, minor mischief, unique dress. Passive: Forgetting, neglecting chores.	Annoyed. Remind, coax.	Temorarily stops behavior. Later repeats behavior or does something else to attract attention.
I am in control or proving no one can control me.	**Power**	Active: Aggressiveness, defiance, disobedience, hostility. Passive: Stubbornness, resistance.	Angry, provoked. Fight power with power or give in.	If parent fights, teen intensifies or submits with "defiant compliance" **If parent gives in, teen stops.
I hurt others as I feel hurt. I don't feel loved or lovable	**Revenge**	Active: Hurtfulness, rudeness, violence, destructiveness. Passive: Staring hurfully at others.	Deeply hurt. Retaliate.	Seeks further revenge by intensifying attack or choosing another weapon.
I convince others not to expect anything from me. I am unable and helpless.	**Display of inadequacy**	Passive only: Quitting easily, avoiding trying. Being truant or dropping out of school. Escaping through	Despairing, hopeless, discouraged. Agree with teen that nothing can be done. Give up. (With drug abuse, may take teen for help.)	

Additional Goals***

I create excitement.	**Excitement**	Avoiding routine. Showing interest in alcohol, other drugs, promiscuous sex, daredevil sports, exciting events, and activities.	Nervous, angry, hurt. What will happen next? Is on guard. May share excitement about positive endeavors.	Resists or continues exciting misbehavior. (May become power contest.)
I have widespread peer acceptance.	**Peer acceptance**	Constantly attempting to obtain widespread peer acceptance.	Approval (if parent agrees with choice of friends). Worried, anxious (if disapproves of friends). Try to get teen to seek new friends.	Resists or continues to see friends. (May become power contest.)
I am the best at everything (or at least better than most).	**Superiority**	Striving for best grades, most honors. Putting down parents and others. Using superior talents against others.	Approval, inadequacy. Praise. Attempt to put teen in his or her place.	Continues striving. Continues putting down others to defend own self-image.

*Most examples of misbehavior given in this column may also be used for the other goals. The only way you know the goal of your teen's misbehavior is to examine the consequences: 1)how you feel when the teen misbehaves, and 2)what happens when you attempt to correct your teen.
**Teen complies only enough to get by, but not to parent's satisfaction.
***These goals can exist outside or inside the parent-teen relationship. Active behavior is usually used to pursue the goals. Although excitement, peer acceptance, and superiority can be pursued as positive goals, examples here present ways in which they serve as negative, irresponsible goals.

Figure 3.3. The goals of teen misbehavior. From *Systematic Training for Effective Parenting of Teens* (STEP/Teen: *Parenting Teenagers* by Dinkmeyer and McKay, 1990, American Guidance Service, Inc., Circle Pines, MN 55014-1796. Reproduced with permission.

Goals are subjective, created, and unconscious. The child or teen is not always aware of the goal. The goal directs the individual's responses and can be seen in cognitive and emotional components. In identifying the student's goals, check the reactions of both the teacher and student. The adult's reaction to the misbehavior is a significant clue toward understanding the goal of the misbehavior.

Goals of misbehavior are an essential part of consultation. Although the initial symptoms may be general, further discussion creates specific misbehavior incidents. Assessment of the misbehavior incidents creates the solutions.

An additional advantage of the goals approach in consultation is its concreteness. Consultees often want specific information about specific incidents. Goals of misbehavior are effective means of engaging consultees at their level of interest. Although behavioral, the approach goes beyond behaviors to beliefs and alternatives.

3. The Individual Is Constantly Striving for Significance.

Individuals strive for success. This goal is part of an individual's perceived (objectively or subjectively) feeling of being less than others and a need to become more than those around oneself.

This goal has its roots in our early and formative years. We are born as helpless individuals, truly dependent upon the caring and attention of others to survive. In many ways, an accurate perception is that one is "less than" others. As we grow, we seek to become equal to those around us, while seeking a unique place in that group.

In contrast to theories which emphasize the "push" of events from the past, Adlerian Psychology recognizes the "pull" of the future. The significance of behavior lies in terms of the consequences, or how the student is seeking to be known. The concern is less with the actual behavior, and more with emphasis on the direction in which the individual is moving. This movement is the striving for significance.

Consultants and consultees benefit from a concrete visualization of this process. For example, the consultant can ask the consultee to imagine the student wearing a T-shirt. If the T-shirt's message was the student's belief, what might it say? *"I want attention"* or "I *want to give up*" are some of the messages students wear.

To create a "flip-side" to these beliefs, the imagined T-shirt can be turned inside out. Here we find the alternatives for the teacher. *"I want attention"* becomes *"catch me being good"* and *"I want to give up"* becomes *"I need lots of encouragement."*

Expectations for the future are powerful. When one works with "where the person is headed" (goal), the involvement is deeper and more significant than attempting to only deal with present behaviors. The consultant is working with "where you will be going, and what you will be doing," in addition to "what you are feeling right now." The striving for significance becomes a motivating force. We do not seek to be significant in the same way, but we all seek to establish a sense of importance. The striving for significance is consistent with the four and seven goals of misbehavior. The student is looking for a place in the classroom. Therefore, the consultant asks the question, *"How is the child seeking to become significant, or known, in this classroom?"*

4. All Behavior Has Social Meaning.

Students act in a social context. Behaviors are for the "benefit" of peers and adults. If a student seeks to attract attention, others must pay attention if the goal is to succeed. Behavior does not operate in a vacuum. It is intended to have an impact on others.

Behavior is influenced by the consequences and reactions of other people. The social meaning of behavior can be discovered in the interactions between the teacher and student, and the student and peers.

5. We Always Have a Choice.

The student creatively interacts with the environment. Behavior is not only reactive or responsive to an external stimulus. Each individual has the capacity to respond creatively. Behavior is never understood solely within the framework of stimulus-response (S-R). It is understood in terms of a S-O-R (stimulus - organism - response). The person (organism) is exercising a choice or decision.

Teachers and parents may not, at first, understand this idea. If a child's goal or purpose is not understood by the adult, it is maintained or reinforced by the adult's behavior. This can increase the teacher's or parent's frustration. A misbehavior can grow stronger rather than weaker. The objective response to a misbehavior is part of the solution. The unique meaning and significance which each individual derives from the misbehavior is also part of the solution. This is part of the process of empathy, the ability to see how it looks from the other person's point of view.

Consultants model empathy for the consultee's feelings and behaviors. This gives an example for the consultee to take to other relationships. Each individual student has learned to perceive life through a personal set of "filtered glasses." The glasses have been shaped according to previous experiences. More importantly, the glasses have been shaped according to the meaning the student has given to events. Through events and the interpretation the child has given to these events, a set of personal beliefs are developed. These beliefs are the basis for the child's interaction with others.

For example, the child may believe that *"people are unfair to me."* Based on this belief, the child expects people to be unfair, and acts accordingly. It is okay, in turn, to be unfair to others. Have people been unfair to this child? The facts are irrelevant. Understand the subjective perception human beings exercise in their interpretation of events. The response to a stimulus is influenced by the individual's beliefs.

6. Belonging Is a Basic Need.

The first group is the family. The second group is often a day-care, nursery, school, or similar peer setting. The "socialization" process of day-care centers, prekindergartens, nursery schools, and elementary schools is the setting for each child's search to belong in the group. The process of finding a place in the classroom group is continuous. Classrooms change from year to year, even day to day. Students grow and exercise their rights as unique individuals. Adolescents have the challenge of finding a place with peer groups. Even the popular high school quarterback is faced with the process of finding another way to belong within the collegiate community, or other group to which he must gain a feeling of belonging. One never graduates from the need to belong within the group.

Belonging in the classroom can be illustrated in the four goals of misbehavior. What explains the class clown, the class bully, or other seemingly undesirable positions? Using private logic and subjective perception, the child decides upon his/her best chance at a unique place in the group. An unwritten rule which can explain seemingly poor behaviors is, "It is better to be notorious than unnoticed!"

Even passive behaviors which seem to put a child at arms length from other students are efforts to establish a unique place in the group. Rudolf Dreikurs often told a story of the hermit who lived two miles outside a small European village. The village burned completely to the ground, and the inhabitants decided to move elsewhere. The hermit then moved two miles outside the new village.

7. Understanding Behavior Is Based on Idiographic, Not Nomothetic Laws.

In understanding human behavior, principles of an idiographic nature (principles that apply to the individual's unique life-style) are of more concern than those of a nomothetic nature (laws that apply generally). Normative group descriptions cannot be universally applied to the individual. While knowing about the average ten-year-old is interesting, that type of data cannot be translated immediately into corrective procedures and practice.

Nomothetic laws do not lend much help in understanding the behavior of the individual from that individual's point of view. Commonly held beliefs such as "the terrible two's" or "all nine-year-olds..." are less useful than beliefs based in observations of a specific two or nine year old's behaviors. Consultants look at both how the individual appears to self, and how that person appears to others.

8. Look at Use, Not Potential.

Many students have been cursed by the label "underachiever." The attributes a person possesses are less important than what that person decides to do with the endowment. We can only deal with what is, not what isn't. Ability cannot be equated with interest. If a child has "high potential" but the potential is not reflected in grades, what is accomplished by telling the child that he or she is not living up to potential?

An individual may choose to not live up to specific capacity for subjective reasons:

Cathy was the third child from a family with musical interests and abilities. When she entered the fourth grade, her parents placed her in the band. She soon was a disruptive force in the band class; the teacher sent a note home saying, "Cathy has to learn to cooperate, or she will have to quit band." Her parents were mystified; Cathy had often imitated her older siblings and had been interested in band. However, they were able to learn that band was held at the same time as physical education, and she didn't want to miss P.E.

What the child does with ability is important. What that maximum ability might be is less important. This is an example of looking at the use, not the potential.

9. Social Interest Is the Indicator of Mental Health.

The development of social interest is crucial for the individual's mental health. Social interest can be defined as the ability to cooperate with others. As consultants, we express this ability in our consultation relationships. Teachers and parents can express confidence in the child's ability to develop social interest.

This ability can be encouraged by specific beliefs about students. Although presented as teacher beliefs about students, the following four ideas equally apply to other relationships:

- I believe students can make decisions;

- I am equal, not more or less than others;

- I believe in mutual respect; and

- I am human. I have the "courage to be imperfect."
  (Dinkmeyer, McKay, & Dinkmeyer, 1980, p. 43)

DISCIPLINE

Many consultees present problems which involve discipline situations. Discipline is an integral part of the schools. Many surveys and public opinion polls rate it as the biggest challenge in our schools.

We believe discipline is an educational process. The consultant teaches the consultee an approach (or theory) to discipline. In turn, the consultee uses this approach with the third party. Often this means the school counselor teaches the teacher how to work with students.

In recent years, a wide variety of systems have been offered to schools which focus on a specific set of rules for more effective discipline. This approach may not be as effective as the system we propose.

The discipline system we advocate uses **natural** and **logical consequences**. In contrast to punishment, consequences are an educational process which capitalizes on the student's inherent tendency to **choose** behaviors. With properly applied consequences, no choices are "bad." Each choice is a learning experience.

The differences between punishment and consequences are expressed in Figure 3.4.

NATURAL AND LOGICAL CONSEQUENCES

When consultees present discipline situations, natural and logical consequences usually apply. In this section, natural and logical consequences are defined and examples are presented.

Children learn and grow through the use of natural and logical consequences. Consequences represent the reality of the social order (**logical consequences**) or the natural course of events without outside interference (**natural consequences**).

What are natural consequences? Staying up late, you feel tired the next morning. Getting caught in a rainstorm without an umbrella, you get wet. Forgetting to eat, you feel hungry. These examples show the natural order of the world. No one has made you tired, wet, or hungry. It is just the way the world works.

What are logical consequences? Students who throw food clean it up. If you fight at recess, you lose a recess (and have the chance to try again). If you do not turn in a paper at an established deadline, you get a zero. These examples show the **logical** relationship between the deed and the discipline. No one has "made" the student throw food, fight, or forget. And the relationship between the behavior and the consequence is a logical one.

Additional examples of logical consequences may be helpful. If the child writes on the wall, clean it up. Forget gym shoes, play the game in socks. This is not another name for punishment. Dreikurs and Gray (1968) indicated five fundamental differences between logical consequences and punishment.

1. Logical consequences express the reality of the social order, not of the person. Punishment expresses the power of personal authority.

2. Logical consequences are logically related to the misbehavior; punishment rarely is.

3. Logical consequences imply no element of moral judgment; punishment often does.

(Continued on page 80)

Major Differences Between Punishment and Logical Consequences

PUNISHMENT			LOGICAL CONSEQUENCES		
Characteristics	Underlying Message	Likely Results	Characteristics	Underlying Message	Likely Results
1. Emphasis on power of personal authority.	Do what I say because I say so! I'm in charge here!	Rebellion. Revenge. Lack of self-discipline. Sneakiness. Irresponsiblity.	1. Emphasis on reality of social order.	I trust you to learn to respect yourself and the rights of others.	Self-discipline. Cooperation. Respect for self and others. Reliability.
2. Rarely related to the act; arbitrary.	I'll show you! You deserve what you're getting!	Resentment. Revenge. Fear. Confusion. Rebellion.	2. Logically related to misbehavior; makes sense.	I trust you to make responsible choices.	Learns from experience.
3. Implies moral judgments.	This should teach you! You're bad!	Feelings of hurt, resentment, guilt, revenge.	3. No moral judgment. Treats student with dignity.	You are a worthwhile person!	Learns behavior, may be objectionable (not to self).

Punishment			Logical Consequences		
4. Emphasizes past behavior.	This is for what you did—I'm not forgetting! You'll never learn!	Feels unable to make good decisions. Unacceptable in eyes of teacher.	4. Concerned with present and future behavior.	You can make your own choices and take care of yourself.	Becomes self-directed and self-evaluating.
5. Threatens disrespect, either open or implied.	You'd better shape up! No one in *my* class acts like that!	Desire to get even. Fear. Rebellion. Guilt feelings.	5. Voice communicates respect and good will.	It's your behavior I don't like, but I still like you!	Feels secure in teacher's respect and support.
6. Demands compliance.	Your preferences don't matter! You can't be trusted to make wise decisions!	Defiant compliance. Plans to get even another time. Destruction of trust and equality.	6. Presents a choice.	You can decide.	Responsible decisions. Increased resourcefulness.

Figure 3.4. Major differences between punishment and logical consequences. From *Systematic Training for Effective Teaching* (STET): *Teacher's Handbook* by Dinkmeyer, McKay, and Dinkmeyer, 1980, American Guidance Service, Inc., Circle Pines MN 55014-1796. Reproduced with permission.

4. Logical consequences are concerned only with what will happen now; punishment, with the past.

5. Consequences are invoked with a friendly voice; punishment with anger—either open or concealed.

In punishment, perhaps the child who forgets gym shoes would be asked to stay after school or write a paper about the importance of remembering. Logical consequences relate to the act. The child is motivated through the reality of life and not the mandate of an authority.

A good relationship between the teacher and child is an essential part of a consequence-based discipline system. A good relationship allows both students and teachers to understand and accept the consequences before they are applied. In a poor relationship, such as when a power conflict exists, the logical consequences turn into punishments.

The consequences must be applied consistently. The child must understand the logical consequences. The teacher needs to be patient and allow time for the behavior to diminish. A misbehavior will not necessarily disappear immediately.

No patent formulas exist for using logical consequences. Each child and situation must be viewed as unique. The individual child and the goal must be considered.

COMPREHENSIVE DISCIPLINE

A comprehensive approach to discipline is an educational process. The consultant must continue to offer the consultee opportunities to work with the consultant so that this education proceeds with an emphasis on **prevention**, not only remediation.

Students can be involved in the discipline process by a variety of methods which seek to involve their cooperation and collaboration. For example, a process as simple as asking students for their ideas on the order in which some materials are to be studied is a discipline method. This is an idea which most consultees do not, initially, consider "discipline." But it is part of a comprehensive approach which understands the theory behind effective discipline.

Some ideas which contribute to this discipline process include student involvement in issues such as

- time spent on certain topics,
- ways to study these topics,
- the order of study,
- methods of evaluation,
- activities and projects,
- committees and small groups,
- classroom jobs, and
- seating arrangements.

For example, one teacher reports she has had increased cooperation by asking students which examples in a workbook they will be doing. Instead of telling students *"Do the first 10 problems on page 143,"* this teacher says *"Do any ten problems on page 143."*

Comprehensive discipline is more than consequences or choices offered in a preventive mode. At the point of misbehavior, the teacher has several options. First, teachers and consultants should seek to understand the purpose, or goal, of the misbehavior. Goal diagnosis, discussed earlier in this chapter, is a vital clue in the teacher's response. In addition to the directives offered through goal diagnosis, four other approaches can be used:

1. **Reflective listening**—this will be presented in Chapter 4. It would be most appropriate for the goals of revenge or display of inadequacy.

2. **I-Messages**—also discussed in Chapter 4, the approach allows the teacher to communicate constructively with the student.

3. **Exploring alternatives**—helps decide whether the problem at hand is a student problem, a shared problem (teacher and student), or a teacher problem.

4. **Natural and logical consequences**

These four approaches to discipline are presented in Figure 3.5. (See pages 84 and 85.)

SUMMARY

Consultants function from their own frame of reference. This approach can be enhanced by an understanding of an effective practical psychology. The Adlerian approach offers such a theory for the consultant. Although simple, the approach allows the consultant to engage the consultee and understand those who concern the consultee in both simple and complex situations.

This theory is comprehensive. Solutions to problems come from the consultant's thorough knowledge of the theory. Adlerian psychology has these elements, including the four goals of misbehavior, the concept of motivation through encouragement, and the holistic approach to the individual. The theory, including an approach to discipline, has been outlined in this chapter.

REVIEW QUESTIONS

1. What are two ineffective beliefs about behavior, and how would they hamper a consultation relationship?

2. Give two effective beliefs about human behavior.

3. What are the key differences between a consultation and counseling relationship?

4. Cite two of the nine ideas about behavior, and compare them with your prior ideas about behavior.

5. What do the authors mean by a discipline "system"?

6. Besides natural and logical consequences, what other approaches to discipline can be used by the consultant?

Effective Approaches to Classroom Challenges

Approach	Purpose	Example
Reflective listening.	Communicating understanding of students' feelings about problems they face.	"You feel very sad because your friend says he doesn't like you anymore."
I-message.	Communicating your feelings to students about how their behavior affects you.	(To the class) "When you are not interested in my lesson, I feel very discouraged because I've worked hard to prepare it."
Exploring alternatives.	Helping students decide how to solve a problem they own or negotiating agreements with students for teacher-owned problems.	"What are some ways you could solve your problem?" Or, "How could we settle our disagreement?"
Natural and logical consequenses.	Allowing students within limits to decide how they will behave and permitting them to experience the results of their decisions.	Natural: Students who fight may get hurt. Logical: Students who fight go to the talk-it-over area.
Giving permission to misbehave.	Doing the unexpected by permitting misbehavior under certain conditions.	A student who swears is invited to go to a corner of the room to practice swearing.

Acknowledging the student's power.	Admitting defeat or vulnerability in an effort to defuse the student's attempt to overpower, get revenge, or show superiority.	"You've proved your point. I can't force you to work."
Creating alternatives: turning a minus into a plus.	Channeling misbehavior and mistaken goals in constructive directions.	The student who uses humor to disrupt can be put in charge of a comic classroom play.

Figure 3.5. Effective approaches to classroom challenges. From *Systematic Training for Effective Teaching* (STET): *Teacher's Handbook* by Dinkmeyer, McKay, and Dinkmeyer, 1980, American Guidance Service, Inc., Circle Pines MN 55014-1796. Reproduced with permission.

REFERENCES

Cater, M.K. (1992). *Action guide for effective discipline in the home and school.* Munice, IN: Accelerated Development.

Dinkmeyer, D., & McKay, G. (1989). *The parent's handbook* (3rd ed.). Circle Pines, MN: American Guidance Service.

Dinkmeyer, D., & McKay, G. (1990). *Parenting teenagers* (2nd ed.). Circle Pines, MN: American Guidance Service.

Dinkmeyer, D., McKay, G., & Dinkmeyer, D., Jr. (1980). *Systematic training for effective teaching.* Circle Pines, MN: American Guidance Service.

Dinkmeyer, D., Dinkmeyer, D., Jr., & Sperry, L. (1987). *Adlerian counseling and psychotherapy* (2nd ed.). Columbus, OH: Merrill.

Dreikurs, R., & Gray, L. (1968). *Psychology in the classroom.* New York: Harper and Row.

Painter, G., & Corsini, R.J. (1990). *Effective discipline in the home and school.* Muncie, IN: Accelerated Development.

Chapter 4

INDIVIDUAL CONSULTATION

In this chapter, you will learn:

- basic consultation procedures,
- how to use teachers as resources,
- the helping relationship, and
- techniques for creating an effective relationship.

BASIC PROCEDURES FOR INDIVIDUAL CONSULTING

The consultant must have a clear perception of the consultation task when working with consultees. The task is to help the consultee to become more aware of inner resources and more sensitive to beliefs which prevent more effective functioning. *Consultants are agents for change and facilitators of human potential.* The ability to make the system more open, dynamic, and sensitive to feedback is essential.

The "system" is the set of relationships among all persons in the school building. Each person interacts with others, with varying degrees of skill and success. The consultant must assess the role and expectation of four major elements of the school system:

1. the role and expectations of the principal;

2. the role and expectations of the teacher, particularly about or in their relationships with the students;

3. the role and expectations of the parents; and

4. the role and expectations of the consultant within this system.

The consultant understands theories and procedures, and develops a collaborative relationship with the staff and parents. Cooperation and an equal commitment toward changing the status quo of the system are elements of the relationship. Working within the system, the consultant creates procedures which offer education, insight, and skill to consultees. The consultant essentially changes the system.

Consulting is similar to counseling. It is another type of helping relationship. **Consulting is different in that its original focus is on the consultee's concern with the client.** If consulting is to be effective, it will be based upon empathy, open communication, commitment, encouragement, and other essential components of counseling. The consultant must have counseling skills which lead to a collaborative relationship.

The collaborative relationship is based upon fundamental beliefs about people and how one facilitates change in behavior, attitudes, and beliefs. Consultation is enhanced by cooperative problem-solving approaches and is impeded by specialist/teacher or superior/inferior methods. The teacher is not someone who needs to be "advised" but rather "consulted". The consultee's concern is not solved by a superficial approach which suggests that the consultant has all of the answers and the task of the consultee is to listen attentively and apply the answers. Teachers need more than ideas. Consultants help individuals integrate new ideas with their beliefs and emotions.

The consultant is not expected to "play expert," even though this may be ego-inflating. Pupil personnel specialists who are always engaged in "crises" are often those whose life-styles seek excitement and who are concerned with being important and keeping others dependent. Consultants must be aware of their beliefs and values to facilitate this awareness in others.

The consultant shares ideas with other staff members. The consultant has a useful understanding of human behavior, group dynamics, and communications. Skills must be internalized by administration, teachers, and parents if education is to facilitate human potential and promote social responsibility.

To receive a request for help with a problem can be flattering. To think that we might be able to provide a ready answer and solve the problem for the consultee can be exhilarating. This is a trap the consultant must avoid. To avoid this and other traps, consultants must understand basic issues such as who is the client, who initiates the consultation, and basic strategies for effective consultation.

IS IT COUNSELING OR CONSULTATION?

The relationship between the counselor and teacher (or parent, or administrator) can be difficult if not clarified. These simple rules help to understand the differences between counseling and consultation.

Consultation is

when the main focus of the relationship is a third person (often a student), and when the relationship is characterized by collaboration on ways to help this third person.

In consultation, the counselor is a consultant and the other adult (teacher, parent, or administrator) is the consultee.

Counseling is

when the main focus of the relationship is the person seeking the help, and

when the relationship is characterized by collaboration on ways to help the person seeking the help. While a third person may be discussed, the goal of the relationship is focused on the help-seeker.

In counseling, although the terms may seem redundant, the counselor is a counselor and the person seeking the help is the client.

IS IT CRISIS, REMEDIAL, OR DEVELOPMENTAL?

Consultations can be divided into three types, dependent upon the unique characteristics of the events surrounding the start of the consultation.

Developmental Consultation

Developmental consultation is perhaps the most preferred type. No crisis situation exists and a major goal is to create a learning experience for the consultee, which transfers to the third parties. This is the type of relationship we discuss in Chapters 5, 6, and 7. Developmental strategies include teacher and parent education groups, classroom guidance activities, and other opportunities for personal and professional growth.

Remedial Consultation

In remedial consultation, as the name implies, some crisis or extreme situation will occur unless steps are taken to prevent the crisis. Intervention strategies are devised so that the situation improves.

Crisis Consultation

In crisis consultation, an extreme or emergency situation has occurred, and the consultant is asked to respond. This is often limited to a "band-aid" or "firehouse" approach. Stress levels may be high, and the willingness of the consultees may be either very high or very resistant.

Identification of Purpose

The consultant, at the beginning of consultation, understands differences and detects the optimum conditions for effective change. While change is possible at any time, developmental consultation has, in general, more core conditions which contribute to effective change.

WHO IS BEING HELPED?

Some approaches to consultation make a point of differentiating between the consultee and the third party. With this approach to consultation, the third party is the one who is being helped.

We do not believe the consultee is an immovable, inflexible conduit through which suggestions to change the third party are delivered. If consultation is to be effective, the consultee must look at the part played in the relationship with that third party. If the willingness to change is very small, the chances of change in that third party are diminished.

Yet many teachers and parents come to the consultation relationship looking only for ways to change the third party. The consultee's attitude can be understood in the context of the theoretical approach outlined earlier in this book.

WHO INITIATES THE CONSULTATION?

Consultation is initiated either by (1) the consultant, (2) the consultee, or (3) someone else in the system.

Self-initiated consultation (#2) is perhaps the most desirable initiation. It suggests a high level of motivation and subsequent willingness to change. If the counselor makes the availability of consultation known, it may increase the number of self-referrals.

Other-referred consultation (#1 and #3) may be more difficult to initiate. The counsultee does not yet know they are supposed to have this relationship. In this case, the consultant should have a general strategy for initiating the consultation.

In general, we suggest the consultant approach the situation as a listener, not a deliver of ultimate truths or responsibilities. A person is more likely to enter the consultation relationship when the consultant, in fact, does listen to situations. Contrast these two approaches to initiating consultation:

1. "The principal said we should talk about the problems you've been having with Stephanie. What would be a good time for you?"

2. "How are things going this year?"

The second approach may seem more vague, but in fact is an invitation to share experiences. The second approach is an **open question. Closed questions** such as "When can we meet?" can put people on the defensive.

This approach is particularly effective with those whom you may have had no prior relationship, such as parents. The initiation of consultation through a threatening, impersonal phone call is not likely to produce satisfying results.

IMPORTANCE OF LIFE-STYLE

Whether consultants are working with parents, teachers, or others in consultation, an essential point is to understand the life-style of all participants.

In Chapter 3 we discussed the importance of understanding the short-term goals of student misbehavior. Equally important is to understand the longer-term goals of behavior and misbehavior.

This long-term movement and behavior is called a **life-style**, a set of learned and chosen beliefs about how to treat others in relationships. The consultant should be aware of the value of this life-style concept in consultation as it affects the three parts of the consultation relationship; student, teacher (consultee), and consultant.

The life-style does not come out of any specific experience, but, instead, from the continual repetition of the approach used to cope with the tasks of life. Each person adopts certain means which facilitate his or her life plan. As these experiences confirm our anticipation, the style of life, or decisions, is confirmed. This occurs during the first six years of life.

When a person is apparently behaving inappropriately, an important point to remember is that the behavior does make sense to the *behaver*, if not the observers! Each of us makes our own experiences, and our own experiences make sense to us. This has profound impact when working in consultation relationships, because two parties are talking about the behavior of a third. Therefore three different sets of perceptions are working at once.

First, the student often is presented by the consultee as a series of anecdotes or behaviors which may seem confusing. If we understand the unity or pattern to these incidents, we are uncovering the life-style. Focusing on one or two confusing incidents will not help. If we can make a statement about the movement of the student, we are identifying a life-style. For example, "Dean is often discouraged and therefore does not try very hard" may summarize a series of incidents and reflects his life-style which is "I am not capable, life is a series of challenges I can't complete; therefore, I will not try to do any of them."

Knowledge of the child's style of life is important, but not essential. Understanding the short-term goals of misbehavior is equally effective. In extreme situations, understanding the child's total life-style can be helpful (this approach is discussed later in this chapter).

Second, the life-style of the teacher or consultee can be understood in the context of the consultation request. Dinkmeyer, McKay, and Dinkmeyer (1980) have identified five common teaching beliefs which impair effectiveness with students. These five are summarized in Figure 4.1 as statements frequently expressed and the comparable beliefs.

Statement	Belief
I must control	control
I am superior	superiority
I am entitled; you owe me	entitlement
I must be perfect	perfection
I don't count; others are more important than I	feeling less than others

Figure 4.1. Five common teaching beliefs.

Each of these beliefs may express itself in specific teacher behaviors, and the resultant student reactions. Teachers who believe they must control the classroom may report to the consultant situations in which the classroom is "hard to control." The following example shows how a life-style expresses itself consistently in all areas.

Mr. Dowling requested a meeting with a school counselor on a consultation basis. He first asked whether this would affect his job performance review, whether the principal would be notified, and whether he could terminate the consultation at his discretion. When these issues were resolved, the presenting problem was a lack of mutual respect in the 8th grade classroom. Students were causing trouble and Mr. Dowling was not sure how to control the situation.

Similar incidents could be presented to illustrate the beliefs of superiority, entitlement, perfection, and feeling less than others. These identifiers are simply a shorthand way of expressing a direction the person usually heads through life. While heading in that direction, certain encounters are sure to follow, and they reflect the chosen direction or belief. One would expect to have dehydration challenges if headed through the desert, and mildew if moving through the rain forest. Some situations are predictable and come with the territory.

Finally, the life-style of the consultant is a critical part of the consultation relationship. We have established the important characteristics of the helping profession: the ability to examine one's motives, and the ability to understand one's movement through life. What do you bring to the consultation relationship?

BELIEFS IN RELATIONSHIPS

Several beliefs are often found in helping relationships. The following three beliefs are examined in detail, and reflect some of the possible life-style combinations a consultant can bring to the relationship. As with all life-styles, there are assets and liabilities.

Control

Consultants who are interested in control may have assets as problem solvers and organizers, and may be good at data collection. The effort or need to control, however, may present challenges when one considers the nature of the consultation relationship. If three parties are involved, and only two are present at the meetings, then to control the third party from a distance is difficult.

Logic is often another strength of the control approach to life-style. The ability to identify misbehavior by going through the anecdotes, the feelings, the reactions, and student reactions may be easier to follow for this person. However, the strength of logic may be impeded by the relative lack of sensitivity to affect or feelings. If you are strong on control, you may be able to identify the content in a person's statements, but more effort may be needed to identify an accurate feeling.

A major area of potential conflict for the control life-style is power. Because to control is important, then those situations where one is not in control, or powerless, are the most challenging. Consultation provides many opportunities to be "out of control." For this person, the issue of giving control or power to the consultee is a major step in establishing the relationship.

Miss Medlock has taught for 22 years in the same building. She literally has the children of the children she taught years ago. From this perspective, she accurately states "I don't understand how children today can be so disrespectful. When I began teaching, I was respected because I was a teacher. Now, it almost seems a game to see if they can get me angry!"

Perfection

A belief that mistakes are deadly, and therefore must be avoided at all costs, can cloud the consultant's view of the relationship. This perfectionistic approach may hamper the consultant's ability to make recommendations or accept progress by the consultee.

One of the relative strengths of this approach is the commitment to high standards. Expressions of this can be found in extensive reading, comprehensive publicity, and dedication to identifying new resources. Perfectionists have even been described as "type A" personalities, or "ash-tray cleaners and pillow fluffers." Behind this humorous description is a life-style dedicated to getting something exactly right. In a consultation relationship, many opportunities occur for things to go wrong.

Mrs. Selby has worked with the consultant on three previous occasions. Progress has been made and there have been substantive changes in the classroom. When she comes to the fourth session, she is visibly discouraged: "Things were going so well, and today was just terrible. It seems I am back to square one." The consultant listened and worked with Mrs.

Selby, helping her to realize that "setbacks" are part of human behavior and not indications of total failures. Mrs. Selby has high standards, and interpreted the most recent problems as the sum and total of the entire consultation experience.

Need to Please

The helping professions have an abundance of individuals who express this life-style. They are sensitive to others' needs, tuned in to what others want. This can be both an asset and a liability.

The liability presents itself when the consultant does not say "no." The following example demonstrates this pitfall:

Mrs. Sampras was asked to serve as a consultant to a neighboring school district, as there were issues which prevented the local counselor from serving as a consultant. She agreed, and devoted an afternoon each week to this task. Once she began, it became clear that much work needed to be done. She began to set aside two afternoons a week, gave consultees her telephone number so she could be reached at other times, and offered to see many of the consultee's students on an individual basis. It became difficult to keep up with the work at her regular school, but she never said " no" to the commitment she made.

The last sentence of the example gives us the situation from Mrs. Sampras' point of view—this was a commitment, and it would be letting people down if she pulled back. Whether true or not, it looked that way to this consultant.

The value of life-style as a consultation concept is wide ranging. Additional discussions of this concept are found in Dinkmeyer, McKay, and Dinkmeyer (1980) and Dinkmeyer, Dinkmeyer, and Sperry (1987).

CONSULTEE LIFE-STYLES: SIMPLIFIED PERCEPTIONS

Everyone has a life-style, and understanding this concept is always helpful in the consultation relationship. We have found that many consultants lack the theoretical basis for a strong understanding of the Adlerian life-style approach. However, all consultants can have a simplified understanding of life-style. The following life-style ideas are expressed as simplified beliefs. These are beliefs often held by consultees. Following each belief is a corresponding representative statement from a parent:

- I must be in control— "When I get my hands on him, he won't be a problem in the classroom anymore. This has gone on too long."

- I must win— "I'm tired of fighting with him, so whatever ideas you have to beat his system is fine by me."

- I am superior— "Who told you to call me? What right do you have to tell me how to raise my children?"

- I must be right— "I've found that my methods are working with him at home, so whatever happens at school isn't following my system."

- I am entitled— "His father is away on military duty and I'm home alone with three kids. It's all I can do to keep our heads above water."

- I must be comfortable— "I don't care what you do with him at school, it's fine by me."

Teacher as Resource

If the consultant has other relationships with teachers, consultation can be clouded by prior perceptions. For example, a school counselor can be a consultant. But prior to this relationship, the counselor has been disciplinarian, in-service chair, or referral resource for individual parent or student problems.

Some teachers enter the consultation relationship passively, waiting for the specialist to solve the problem. The teacher is a critical resource in consultation, not incidental to the problem situation. The consultant must see the teacher's role in the total situation. From this awareness comes the possibility of change.

The teacher brings assets to the consultation situation. A detailed picture of the interaction between the teacher and the child is an asset. The teacher is in the classroom where the interactions are occurring. The teacher provides the consultant with a perception of the causal factors. The consultant must be aware of how the teacher sees the problem. Eventually, the teacher is also the only one who can provide feedback to the consultant regarding the effectiveness of the recommendations.

Teachers are *essential* resources in the consultation process. If the consultant believes effective relationships are questions followed by answers, this resource is lost. If the teacher believes a consultation relationship is a referral for "repair," this resource is lost. This chapter now moves to the key elements in an effective consultation relationship.

Helping Relationship

Consider the nature of the helping relationship. Perhaps the most extensive study of the helping professions has been accomplished by Arthur Combs and his staff at the University of

Florida (Combs et al., 1969). Research by Combs et al. indicated that the basic tool with which the helper works is **self.**

The helping professions are based upon the capacity of the helper to be a problem-solving person. Helpers are able to dialogue with immediate, not delayed, responses. *Communication and human relations skills that process dialogue instantly and meaningfully are at the core of the consulting process.* The consultant must be able to listen to the whole message (cognitive-affective) and facilitate the potential of the consultee.

Teachers present problems from their point of view. Typical responses arise from values, beliefs, purposes, and perceptions. The teacher may be aware of this belief system, but more often it is not in immediate awareness.

The teacher functions on the basis of the current perceptions. If Rocky behaves a certain way out of "meanness," then Rocky is treated as if he were mean. The consultant helps the teacher to develop alternative perceptions and become aware of resources to develop new methods of interacting and responding. The consultant facilitates perception change by emphatically relating to the consultee a perception of his or her beliefs and attitudes. This facilitative confrontation creates awareness, insight, and the opportunity to change beliefs and perceptions.

Teachers are often similar to the computer: dependent upon the data. One of the functions of the consultant is to increase the consultee's understanding and acceptance of new hypotheses and new perceptions, or to make new data available to the consultee. The consultant helps to generate tentative hypotheses and explore alternatives.

We believe behavior is always understood as a consequence of perceptions about the world and self. If one is familiar with the history of the helping professions in the fields of counseling, psychology, and social work, one recognizes that they have frequently tried to change the behavior of significant adults by providing them with additional information. This has traditionally occurred in in-service programs which present new theories, additional observations, or the results of research related to human behavior. For most teachers, this type of approach remains on the periphery of their consciousness. They hear about new ideas, they even consider them as exciting, possible, or plausible, but they do not make an attempt to change. Why? Knowledge alone does not produce a change in behavior. Knowledge is experienced in terms of its personal meaning. If knowledge is presented in a manner that involves the teacher's feelings and attitudes as well as cognitive acceptance, it can be meaningful for the teacher.

The teacher cannot hear about a new approach and be expected to change. This approach is considered in light of present perceptions, beliefs, and attitudes. If we help the teacher explore what might prevent use of this approach, we affect the teacher-student interactions.

In consultation, the problem is compounded. Our beliefs, (our life-style) have an organizing or directing effect upon all of our perceptions. Established beliefs can limit the ability to change behaviors.

Thus, consulting involves becoming concerned with the internal frame of reference of the teacher, child, and consultant. Emphasis on the importance of understanding the child's perceptual field is part of the process. An exaggerated emphasis is, "If the teacher understood the child's perceptions, things would change." This understanding by itself will not bring about change.

One of the most interesting aspects of the Combs et al. research is the recognition that much of the previous research on the helping professions failed to identify efficacious helpers. Prior research was concentrated on symptoms and not causes. In contrast, Combs et al. was concerned with the internal frame of reference of the helper. ***The consultant seeks to understand this internal frame of reference of the consultee.***

In the training of helping professionals we must be concerned with making them more people-oriented. They need to be more concerned about their relationship with the teachers and less concerned with the technical aspects of diagnosis. Combs et al. established that whether the helper perceived the client as able or unable made a considerable difference. The consultant must value the teacher and must communicate that the teacher is a person of worth who is truly concerned with improving the present situation.

This relationship is contrasted with an attitude of professional superiority. Consultants often convey indirectly or nonverbally the message, "Teachers don't understand children," or other attitudes which devalue and degrade teachers. An effective helper always begins by seeing persons in a positive way, as dependable and capable. ***The consultant and consultee are equal collaborators in bringing about change.***

The Combs' et al. study indicated that two characteristics stand out in terms of the helper's perceptions of self. Effective helpers appear to see themselves as identified and involved with persons, and to have a positive view of self.

Combs et al. (1969) suggested why these characteristics are important when they stated:

A positive view of self provides the kind of internal security which makes it possible for persons who possess such views of self to behave with much more assurance, dignity, and straightforwardness. With a firm base of operations to work from, such persons can be much more daring and creative in respect to their approach to the world and more able to give of themselves to others as well. (p. 74)

The person who is confident, spontaneous, and creative in the approach to problem solving communicates these values to the teacher. For example, the consultant is worthy, but does not have to be perfect. Consultants refuse to accept or participate in any myth that assumes the teacher will provide the problem, and the consultant provides the solution.

Combs et al. (1969) suggested:

> The question of methods in the helping professions is not a matter of adopting the "right" method, but a question of the helper discovering the right method for him. That is to say, the crucial question is not "what" method, but the "fit" of the method, its appropriateness to the self of the helper, to his purposes, his subjects, the situation, and so forth. We now believe the important distinction between the good and poor helper with respect to methods is not a matter of his perceptions of methods, per se, but the authenticity of whatever methods he uses. (p. 75)

This research has considerable implication for the type of person the consultant must be and the nature of the helping relationship. The consultant has an impact on the school setting with abilities to deal with the internal frame of reference and uniqueness of each consultee. The consultant considers the uniqueness of the child, the teacher, the setting, and the relationships which are produced in this set of transactions, thereby facilitating growth in all of these areas.

A major problem of ineffective helpers is unauthentic or contrived methods, "put on" for a certain situation. This is communicated to the teacher as incongruent and confusing. Teachers are seldom convinced by someone who suggests the importance of listening, understanding, and accepting the child, but who demonstrates in the consultant relationship failure to listen, understand, and accept others.

To summarize Combs' et al. research, a significant difference exists between effective and ineffective helpers in the following dimensions. Effective helpers are characterized by the following perceptual organization:

A. The general frame of reference of effective helpers tends to be one which emphasizes:

1. An internal rather than an external frame of reference.

2. Concern with people rather than things.

3. Concern with meanings rather than facts and perceptual events.

4. An immediate rather than a historical view of causes of behavior.

B. Effective helpers tend to perceive other people and their behavior as:

1. Able rather than unable.

2. Friendly rather than unfriendly.

3. Worthy rather than unworthy.

4. Internally rather than externally motivated.

5. Dependable rather than undependable.

6. Helpful rather than hindering.

C. Effective helpers tend to perceive themselves as:

1. With people rather than apart from people.

2. Able rather than unable.

3. Dependable rather than undependable.

4. Worthy rather than unworthy.

5. Wanted rather than unwanted.

D. Effective helpers tend to perceive the task as:

1. Freeing rather than controlling.

2. Larger rather than smaller.

3. Revealing rather than concealing.

4. Involved rather than uninvolved.

5. Encouraging process rather than achieving goals.

(Combs et al., 1969, pp. 32-33)

CREATING A STRUCTURE FOR EFFECTIVE CONSULTATION

How does the consultant create an awareness of the consultation opportunity?

1. Faculty meetings, newsletters, and personal visits are opportunities for the entire staff to become aware of the services the consultant can provide.

2. Be available and accessible at teacher locations, and be flexible to respond to requests for assistance.

3. Conduct discussions with the administrator to elicit support for the consultation role.

The best methods for consulting will always depend upon the individuals and the setting. The consultant establishes a procedure that makes consultation visible and readily accessible. Dialogue with the administration helps the system. The administrator's attitude toward consultation is essential. Without this support all efforts will fail.

Consultation exists in an atmosphere where "deficiencies" in relationships are discussed. One must be cautious about procedures in which the teacher requests that the administrator be the consultant. Some administrators recognize that consultation is effective when the teacher talks with a person who has no supervisory or administrative responsibility over his or her professional position.

In summary, consultants must have the following conditions:

1. administrative support,

2. freedom for teachers to seek consultation without administrative supervision, and

3. administrators who do not serve as consultants.

The consultant is available in places where teachers gather before school, during recess, and after school. This may not be the best setting to share concerns and problems. Thus, a consultant has office hours and a schedule with flexibility to accept requests.

Although we stress a systems approach, the efficiency of individual consultation can be established. In later chapters we discuss group methods. In this chapter, the emphasis in on individuals.

Previous discussions have established conditions in which individual consultation is advisable (Brown, Kurpius, & Morris, 1988; Fuqua & Newman, 1985). Fuqua and Newman listed five conditions which we amplify with our comments:

1. *Problems are strictly of an individual nature.* This is often the case when a teacher reports problems with a student.

2. *System interventions are impractical, unlikely, or untimely.* Consultants may be in systems where few seek their services. The system atmosphere may not be conducive to change.

3. *Problem perceptions are limited to individuals.* This is similar to Item 1.

4. *The consultee's work setting is highly resistant to change.* This is similar to Item 2.

5. *Individual change may be more efficient than system-wide change.*

Regardless of the conditions, consultation on an individual basis can be effective.

DIAGNOSTIC STUDENT INTERVIEW

One element of the consultation process may be a brief interview with a student. This interview is not lengthy. The purpose is to establish some impressions about how the student sees the world. It also enables the consultant to check tentative hypotheses.

This interview gathers information and checks impressions. It does not have therapeutic intentions. The consultant conveys to the student interest in the student and in progress in school. The student can talk about self, and the relationship with the teacher, peers, and school tasks.

The interview is structured to understand the child's perceptions. Skilled consultants obtain insight into the life-style. Thus, although we provide suggested topics or questions, the interviewer will be free in the sense that the answers or responses will provide clues as to the most productive areas for investigation.

Some questions that have been found to be particularly useful include the following:

1. Which of your brothers or sisters behaves most like you? How?

2. Which of your brothers or sisters behaves most differently from you? How?

(Questions 1 & 2 provide some insight into how the child sees his or her behavior. They give some understanding of his or her perceptual field. By telling how siblings are alike or different, by implication the child is telling a good deal about self.)

3. What do you like about school? Why?

4. What do you dislike about school? Why?

5. Are there any subjects you particularly like or dislike?

(Questions 3, 4, and 5 provide some insight into how the child perceives school and its requirements.)

6. What do you particularly enjoy doing with mother or father? Why? When you misbehave, who disciplines you, mother or father? How?

7. What do you like to do least with mother or father? Why?

8. Do you have jobs to do at home? Do you usually do them without being reminded?

(Questions 6, 7, and 8 provide some insight into the family atmosphere and the type of relationship that exists in the home.)

9. How do you spend your time when you can do just as you please?

If the relationship with the child is a good one—if he or she is interested and involved in the interview—sometimes additional diagnostic clues can be obtained by asking the child the following questions:

1. If you were going to be in a play or show, what kind of person would you like to pretend to be? Why?

2. If you were going to pretend to be an animal, what animal would you like to be? Why?

3. Which kind of animal would you not like to be? Why?

4. If you had three wishes, and only three, what would you wish for first, second, and third?

These kinds of questions will give some insight into the fantasy life and wishes of the child. The kind of person he or she chooses may not be significant, but the reasons for the choice may provide some clues. One must determine why the person or animal is chosen. For example, if he or she chooses a police officer, we don't know anything about the child's value structure, but if the child tells us the choice of a police officer was because he or she would like to boss others around, instead of helping others, it gives us some idea of the value structure.

The selection of an animal also attains significance only after we have ascertained the reason. A child may choose an alligator, but we should not attempt to guess the reason. Some children may choose alligators because they are vicious and can "get even," while others choose them because they lie in the sun and sleep all day. The consultant must ask the child why he or she chose a particular animal in order to avoid projecting ideas upon the child. The kinds of wishes that are selected also will give some idea of how the child values people and things.

When the consultant has had special training in understanding the use of early recollections, they may be particularly helpful in gaining an impression of the way in which the child views the world. When a child is asked to recall one of the first things he or she can remember happening, either before or after school or during the child's first years of school, these recollections provide some indication of the child's assumptions about life.

The following is an example of a particularly meaningful recollection taken from the case records of an eleven-year-old child who was referred because, although he had above average IQ, he seldom produced in the classroom in line with the teacher's expectations. The consultant asks, "Tell me about the first things you can recall that happened to you, and how you felt about them." The child replied, "I remember when I was five my friends could ride a two-wheeler, but I could only ride a tricycle. I tried to catch up to them but I couldn't. I felt very bad about this." Another recollection: "I would have to do all of my work over. My parents felt I was too small. I felt very unhappy." These recollections give us some insight into some faulty assumptions, such as:

1. I am not as much as others my age.

2. People don't believe I can function as well as I should.

The interview provides the consultant with an opportunity to establish some tentative hypotheses about child behavior. The consultant attempts to ascertain the purpose of the behavior. He or she uses this interview to pose some tentative hypotheses to the child, such as: "Could it be you are behaving the way you are because it keeps the teacher very busy with you?" "Is it possible you don't do your work in school so you can be excused from all requirements?" While the answers the child gives may be significant and often an indication of his or her awareness of the reason for the behavior, they are not all determining. One must look closely for nonverbal signs such as tone of voice, nervous movement of the eyes, facial expressions, and, of course, a roguish smile or twinkle of the eyes which Dreikurs (1967) described as the "recognition reflex."

ADDITIONAL SUGGESTIONS FOR CHANGE

The consultant must be well grounded in an understanding of the psychology of human behavior and the dynamics of classroom interaction. This enables the consultant to provide a variety of corrective techniques which can be tailored to the uniqueness of both the child and the teacher. Some general suggestions which have been found to be very helpful when applied idiographically include the following:

1. Helping the teacher to be aware of the importance of the relationship between self and the child. The consultant could suggest a specific way in which the teacher might change the relationship and indicate how this change, if it is done consistently, may influence the child. The encouragement relationship is basic to the consultation process.

2. Helping the teacher to understand the efficacy of logical consequences in contrast to punishment. For example, the consultant can help the teacher to recognize that if the tardy child does not have the assignment reviewed, the student may learn to come on time. In the same manner, if the child who acts out during instruction is given instruction after the class, the student may learn to be more cooperative.

3. Helping the teacher to avoid rewarding misbehavior. Frequently, the teacher unconsciously helps to maintain the misbehavior. For example, a child is acting up and disturbing the class. Instead of removing the child, which may involve the teacher in a power struggle and may be just what the child is interested in, the teacher should refuse to fight with the student. Instead, dismiss the child at this time and arrange a private session at a later date.

4. Helping the teacher to be aware of the nature of his or her relationship with the children. Some teachers are too kind, and the children run all over them. Other teachers try to be too firm and too tough, and the children only rebel. The consultant can provide the teacher with a more objective observation of the nature of his or her relationships with children. The consultant can help the consultee to see how each relationship must be composed of both kindness and firmness. The kindness will indicate to the children care and respect, while the firmness will indicate self-respect, which in turn elicits the children's respect.

5. Helping the teacher to become aware of the power of the group and group discussion. Since all behavior has a social purpose, behavior can often best be influenced through group discussion. The group can often serve as an excellent diagnostic tool. When the teacher does not know why the child is misbehaving during a group discussion, the consultant may ask the class, "Why do you think Johnny is acting as he is?" Frequently the peers will be very sensitive to the purpose of this misbehavior.

6. Helping the teacher to become more aware of the way in which the child reveals life-style through interactions with others. Nonverbal behavior (smiles, signals, and other facial expressions) may help to reveal the child's psychological movement and the way in which he or she seeks to become significant in the group. Only as the teacher becomes aware of each child's unique life-style can the teacher access procedures for modifying the behavior.

7. Helping the teacher to recognize that one of the most powerful tools for change is the proper utilization of responsibility. Too often teachers give responsibility to the child who has demonstrated responsibility. It is much more useful therapeutically to give responsibility to a child who needs the responsibility to enhance development.

8. Helping the teacher to be free from outmoded approaches for dealing with difficult children. Teachers should be particularly cautious of using schoolwork or assignments as a punishment and should refuse to become involved in the child's attempts to manipulate the teacher. The teacher must become competent in understanding human behavior and motivation.

9. Helping the teacher to understand the child's style of life and to learn to anticipate the child's actions. Often when the teacher is confused, the best response is to do exactly the opposite of what the child expects.

10. Helping the teacher to recognize that talking at the child will not change the behavior. What is often observed is that

teachers tend to talk too much and act too little. The consultant should help the teacher to see how a new relationship and logical consequences are more efficacious.

11. Helping the teacher to develop a classroom council. When considerable difficulty exists within a room, a classroom council can help set limits and rules that will be more acceptable to the total group.

Two Examples of Individual Consultation

Individual consultation requires a number of skills and an awareness of procedures, but it is always based upon the capacity to develop an effective, problem-solving approach with the teacher. The following example illustrates some of the problems encountered in helping teachers to focus on the specific problem and to become aware of their feelings and reasons for behavior.

Each of the consultant's carefully selected leads and responses has a specific purpose.

T = teacher   C = consultant

C1: Could you tell me something about this boy Phil?

T1: Yes, he's in my eighth-grade science class, and he drives me insane.

C2: He really bothers you.
(Hears the feeling)

T2: The worst I've ever had.

C3: Tell me about a specific time.

T3: Every time I start to teach he gets up and walks around the room. Sometimes he just leaves the classroom.

C4: Can you think of one specific incident recently that you could describe?
(Aims to get away from generalizations)

T4: Yes, I was teaching science, and I thought I had a pretty good science lesson prepared. The boys and girls were sitting in a group when all of a sudden Phil starts to cough real loud. I thought maybe he needed to get adrink so I said, "Phil, if you want to get a drink, go ahead." He answered, "Oh no, that's OK." I proceeded to teach, when suddenly he just gets up and leaves my classroom. I asked him, "Where are you going?" Hesaid, "I'm going to get a drink. You said I could." But this was 25 minutes later.

C5: How did you feel when he did this?
(Attempts to see how behavior affects teacher)

T5: I'm always angry whenever he does something like this. He really makes me mad.

C6: What do you do?
(Attempts to identify teacher's response)

T6: I told him to get back to his seat. Sometimes I try to ignore him.

C7: When you tell him to go back, does he go right away?

T7: Oh yes, he's usually pretty good. He might look out the window a few minutes, but he eventually strolls back to his place. I mean he's not bold or anything.

C8: Do you have any idea why he does this?
(Investigates teacher's perception of purpose of behavior)

T8: I think he does it to get my attention. He knows every time he walks around or leaves the classroom I'm going to stop whatever I'm doing and ask him, "What's wrong?" I

think he's really a boy who craves attention.
(Here the teacher describes his home situation, stressing the fact that he has a very tough father.)

C9: What kind of attention do you give him?

T9: Well, I try to spend time with him. I spend time after school. He's on the basketball team, and he's got tremendous potential, but he drives the coaches insane. He doesn't pay attention to what he's doing.

C10: Could we just go back for a minute? You said that when he does this sort of thing you get really mad, and you also said at one point that you ignore him. What would you say is your usual reaction to what he does?

T10: I think he's aware of the fact that he makes me mad.

C11: Do you think he knows he's going to get you angry?
(Attempts to see how child perceives his response)

T11: Well, I don't know if he can see my anger, because I don't ever really yell at him, or scream.

C12: I was thinking that sometimes children, if they know they can get you angry, are really trying to control you. You know, they want to be in charge.
(Poses a tentative hypothesis so teacher can see the relationship between his feelings and child's purpose)

T12: I really think he's a smart boy. He's got a high IQ, and I feel he could do much better in school. I'll give him five or ten science problems, and he'll do maybe two of them for homework. (She then describes his work on similar assignments.) I think he deliberately doesn't do the problems.

C13: And you think he does this to get your attention?

T13; Oh, I think so. If I keep him after school, he's really happy.

C14: And yet the problem seems to be mostly in school. Are there ever times that you think that maybe you give him a little encouragement?
(Attempts to focus on school situation where teacher had problem)

T14: I don't know, I think maybe I'm just very negative against him. I don't see him doing too many things I could praise him for. I can't praise him for burning a kid's hair, or leaving the room, etc. I could try that, though.

C15: It would almost seem that if he wants attention, he could get it another way. He seems to want our attention.
(Creates awareness of how child gets attention)

T15: I could maybe try looking for things. I don't know if I'll find anything, but I could at least try.

C16: I think maybe for the next few days you should give it a try, even if it's just a small thing.

T16: Yes, I really never thought of that. It might be what he needs.

C17: If he could get your attention another way, he wouldn't have to resort to these other things.

In this example it appears that the child was involved in a power struggle with the teacher, but the consultant focused on attention getting as the purpose of misbehavior. The consultant's leads were appropriate, but at C5 and T5 the consultant could have caught the teacher's feeling of anger and explored the possibility of the child's desire to obtain power.

The following example illustrates how the consultant helps the consultee to explore his or her own beliefs:

T: I sent for you to get your help with my student, Ricky.

C: Yes.

T: He appears to be a child who needs some kind of affirmation. He just slugs anybody, anytime, and then chuckles to himself. Basically he appears to be tenderhearted. I really like him a great deal. I want him to be accepted by the other kids. He really wants to be accepted, and it appears to me that he does all these things to get the attention he is looking for. Do you think that is correct, or am I grasping at straws?

C: Do you mean that he wants to be accepted and doesn't know how to go about it?
(Clarifies teacher's belief)

T: Yes, to get this attention without using diabolical means.

C: Sure. Can you give me anything specific that he has done?

T: Somebody goes past his desk, and he takes a lunge at the person, no matter who it might be.

C: How do you feel when this happens?
(Determines feeling in order to clarify purpose of behavior)

T: Well, I feel kind of sorry for the kid. I'd like to see him get along with the others. I've talked to others to see what the problem is, but they can't seem to pinpoint it. They want nothing to do with him.

C: Tell me more about how you feel.

T: I suppose basically I feel sympathetic toward him as he has so many good things about him. He really is tenderhearted. I would like him to be accepted. When we had our first parent-teacher-child conference, he was very quiet.

C: Did you tell the parents why he was so unpopular?
(Fails to explore teacher's belief about Ricky)

T: Yes. His mother was constantly at his defense. This greatly bothered me. The father didn't have much to say. The mother talked all the while. The father seemed to approve of my attitude. I felt I got nowhere with the mother. Later on we had another conference, this time only with the mother. She told me the father berates Ricky all the time. I began thinking his actions toward his peers might be revenge.

C: When he acts this way, what do the other children do? What are the consequences of his behavior?

T: They are varied. There's some laughter, girls feel defenseless, and boys generally ignore him or tolerate him. The girls complain when they have to sit near him.

C: How does he react when he hears these complaints? Does he look satisfied or happy?
(Tries to establish a purpose for action)

T: I think he is perplexed. Outwardly he shows little emotion.

C: Has he ever been mean to you?
(Clarifies idea about Ricky's behavior)

T: No, he never turns on me. I give him plenty to do.

C: From what you have said, he seems to tyrannize only those who are weaker than he is, more or less as his father does to him. I agree with you in thinking his goal is revenge. Do you ever punish him?

T: Sometimes if he is annoying someone near him, I move him away.

C: That really isn't a punishment, just a result of his action. Have you ever talked to him about this?

(Clarifies distinction between logical consequences and punishment)

T: I've said to him, "Tell me about how you act."

C: What did he say?

T: He wants to be accepted. He knows how he acts. Sometimes he says he doesn't know why he acts the way he does.

C: I'd like to make a few suggestions. On one of the better days, talk with him and hypothesize about revenge being his goal of behavior. See what he says and what his reaction might be. See if you can encourage him as you have been doing. Make some observations, and we will discuss Ricky again in a week. What do you think you could do differently with him?
(Attempts to accomplish too much in one lead)

T: I guess I could start to be more aware of my feelings about him.

C: Your feelings, tell me more.

T: I really feel very angry at times, but it is only now that I've recognized it.

C: It's hard to admit this anger towards a child, but it will help us understand the interaction. Do you think you could find some small thing to encourage?

T: He is very helpful during math, and I could notice it.

Individual consulting involves putting counseling skills to use with the consultee to develop awareness, understanding, new relationships, and commitment to new procedures.

SUMMARY

Individual consultation requires skills similar to counseling. The consultant's attitude toward the consultee can be effective or ineffective. A structure for individual consultation requires prior efforts to create a comfortable atmosphere for referrals. Administration must play an important supportive but unobtrusive role.

REVIEW QUESTIONS

1. What is the difference between individual counseling and a consultation relationship?

2. Define differences among a crisis, remedial, and developmental consultation relationship.

3. What role does life-style play in consultation?

4. How can teachers be used as resources?

5. If counseling is a helping relationship, what do the authors mean when they state that consultation also can be a helping relationship?

6. What role does the diagnostic student interview play in consultation?

REFERENCES

Brown, D., Kurpius, D.J., & Morris, J.R. (1988). *Handbook of consultation with individuals and small groups.* Alexandria, VA: Association for Counselor Education and Supervision.

Combs, A., et al. (1969). *Florida studies in the helping professions,* Monograph No. 37. Gainesville, FL: University of Florida Press.

Dreikurs, R. (1967). *Psychodynamics, psychotherapy, and counseling.* Dubuque, IA: Kendall/Hunt.

Dinkmeyer, D., Dinkmeyer, D., Jr., & Sperry, L. (1987). *Adlerian counseling and psychotherapy* (2nd ed). Columbus, OH: Merrill.

Dinkmeyer, D., McKay, G., & Dinkmeyer, D., Jr. (1980). *Systematic training for effective teaching.* Circle Pines, MN: American Guidance Service.

Fuqua, F., & Newman, J. (1985). Individual consultation. *The Counseling Psychologist, 13*(3), 390-395.

Chapter 5

WORKING WITH TEACHERS

In this chapter, you will learn:

- the importance of teacher perceptions,
- the fallacy of the useless triangle,
- effective beliefs for teachers and consultants,
- effective behaviors for teachers and consultants,
- individual consultation techniques,
- effective group procedures, and
- encouragement procedures.

Teachers present challenges to the consultant which are influenced by their "faulty beliefs." The purpose of consultation with teachers is to identify faulty beliefs while offering alternative beliefs and corresponding behaviors for the teacher. If we can focus on beliefs, the behaviors will change in response to our understanding of these beliefs.

Consultation with teachers is the most challenging consultation relationship in the schools. Influencing the learning climate includes teacher consultation. Teachers have a full agenda, including expectations for more effective discipline and higher test scores. This agenda has become job performance criteria for some teachers. Public opinion polls consistently show that discipline is a major concern of teachers, while taxpayers, school boards, and administrators expect better academic performance from children.

TEACHER-CONSULTANT RELATIONSHIP

The relationship between consultant and teacher is collaborative. Attention to the first stage of the relationship with other staff members is crucial. An important aspect is to be seen as a helping partner. Consulting involves understanding the dynamics of human behavior and the feelings, attitudes, and purposes of adults as well as children.

To establish this relationship, the consultant must be perceived by administrators as one who is available to help the significant adults, as well as the children. Many consultants schedule regular consulting sessions with the school administrator. If the principal acknowledges and accepts the importance of a consultation relationship between counselor and teachers, a first step in the process is achieved. The principal also must encourage these consultation relationships. For example, the counselor may be specifically introduced to the teacher by the principal as a teacher resource: a consultant.

The principal realizes that, in order to establish this kind of role with staff, time must be allowed to establish the necessary and sufficient conditions for consultation. The consultant not only must be capable of analyzing concerns and developing recommendations, but also must be capable of assessing teacher strengths and providing encouragement which builds the teacher's self-esteem.

The consultant may spend the first month of the school year becoming acquainted with the administrators, teachers, and parents, both formally and informally. Consultants often schedule individual meetings with each teacher to find out how they may collaborate. Many consultants find that meeting individually with parents is a good use of time (Carlson & Jarman, 1975). Consultants are listeners, becoming aware of perceptions of classrooms, students, and relationships. Classroom observations assess the climate for learning and the problems.

The consultant also identifies the strengths in the system. To be able to develop clearly a systems analysis of the school is very important (Lewis & Lewis, 1989).

A collaborative relationship with staff must precede all other efforts. The consultant must plan a daily schedule to avoid being continually manipulated by "the crisis situation." The real crisis is the need to develop a relationship with teachers which makes it both possible and probable that they will seek the consultant as a helper. One can easily be seduced into rapidly responding to every "crisis." However, this is generally highly unproductive. The crisis referral cannot dominate the daily schedule.

Cultivating a positive relationship with teachers includes specific behaviors. Be accessible and go to the areas where teachers are usually found such as the teachers' lounge. The teachers' lounge is not the place to conduct professional consultation. However, it may be the place where one can break down the artificial barriers that sometimes exist between the specialist and the teacher. Consultants share the professional concerns of teachers. Consultation can sometimes be seen only as child advocacy. Instead, what must be apparent to teachers is that the consultation helps the teacher to accomplish tasks with less personal stress and tension.

Too often the consultant is seen as someone who suggests that the teacher's procedures are ineffective and that treating the child as an individual, or providing more attention or love, will resolve all problems. Teachers often feel that little, if any, understanding is shown of problems that they have in trying to deal with students. An example is the suggestion to provide individualized instruction when both the size of the class and available materials makes this an impossibility.

The consultant must be able to enter the perceptual field of the teacher, to understand the teacher's frame of reference. Teacher beliefs such as *"I must be in control."* or *"I know what is best for children."* may be major deterrents to the change process.

A second grade teacher comes to the consultant asking for help with Ryan, an active boy continually disrupting quiet work times.

> Teacher: *Have you got any ideas about Ryan? He's really causing problems since school began, disrupting work sheet times.*
>
> Consultant: *Maybe you can isolate him — face his desk in the opposite direction.*
>
> Teacher: *I've tried that. He gets a big grin on his face and I feel that he's getting more attention!*

In this example, the consultant is "seduced into the crisis" and first dispenses advice. The consultant has not heard the teacher's concern. The teacher's response gives large clues as to the purpose of Ryan's behavior, but the consultant missed this information while dispensing advice.

To empathize with a teacher in an inappropriate way is easily done, especially when the consultant has taught.

> Teacher: *Have you got any ideas about Ryan? He's really causing problems since school began, disrupting work sheet times.*
>
> Consultant: *Yes, I used to have that problem when I taught fourth grade.*
>
> Teacher: *What did you do?*

An attempt to empathize with the teacher may become an opportunity to dispense advice. No recognition of the current situation—the teacher's frame of reference—has been made. Consultants must ask "*Who is my client?*" In almost all cases the answer should be, "*My client is the person who brought me the problem.*" The consultant helps the consultee, who is the client, to recognize problem ownership. Though the consultee might like to "turn the case over" to the consultant, the consultant helps the consultee see her/his part in the interaction and create an awareness of the opportunity to change the problem situation. A more appropriate response would be:

Teacher: *Have you got any ideas about Ryan? He's really causing problems since school began, disrupting work sheet times.*

Consultant: *You seem really bothered by Ryan. Can you give me a specific example where he did this recently? Tell me what he did, what you did and felt, and then what he did next.*

The consultant does not operate as if the child is the one who is concerned about the problem. In many instances the student does not even think there is a problem. The client is the teacher.

Only through working with the teacher can the teacher's specific concerns be handled. The unmotivated student will not be concerned about the teacher's goals. Pupil personnel services have traditionally confused this issue and have been ineffective. The power to change through diagnosis does not exist. Hence, the classic statement "*I sent Johnny for testing a month ago, and he still isn't any better*" misunderstands the teacher-student relationship.

Jerry seldom gets his arithmetic finished and spends the time talking with another child. This is not something he wants to change. When the teacher seeks a consultant about Jerry, an important point to recognize is that Jerry *does* have a real problem. However, it may not be the same problem the teacher perceives. The problem that can be solved by the consultant and the teacher, working together, is the teacher's relationship with Jerry.

Another point that must be made clear is that one can only change one's own behavior. If Jerry is to change, the teacher must change first. As the teacher functions differently, Jerry will begin to change. This does not imply that the teacher is at fault. Instead, it merely deals with the reality that the teacher must first change if the child is to change.

This strategy recognizes that the teacher is in discomfort, experiencing dissonance, and is therefore ready to change. This approach utilizes concepts of systems theory and realizes change in one part of the system impacts all other parts. Change involves changing both teacher and child perceptions. Contacts with staff members can be developed through formalized procedures, such as presentations at faculty meetings relevant to the consultant role, role-playing demonstrations with teachers which provide some insight into the way in which the consultant functions, and through newsletters from the consultant. A newsletter has been demonstrated to provide an opportunity for in-service contact with faculty. This newsletter could include material about identifying emotional problems, detecting guidance needs, implementing group discussion procedures, handling discipline, or conducting parent interviews.

DISCIPLINE: THE USELESS TRIANGLE

A study by one of the authors has shown that teachers believe parents are the major cause of discipline problems in their classrooms. Our research (Dinkmeyer, Jr., 1980) examined teacher perceptions of discipline problems. Most teachers agreed that discipline (behavioral) problems were in their classrooms; unacceptable behaviors were present that they were unable to change. Further, these teachers saw this student-teacher relationship problem as caused by the parent, poor home environment, and other external factors.

This belief appears to put a third corner, or triangular, framework on the discipline problem. If you believed parents caused Laura's behavior problems, what would you do? Telephoning Laura's parents is certainly consistent with your belief. And this is exactly what teachers in Dinkmeyer's research reported—repeated attempts to contact parents, hoping they would own part of the problem. An important point is to recognize how consistent this teacher behavior is with the current belief and how one's beliefs influence behaviors.

If the teacher cannot create change by parent contact, the teacher may turn to another adult, the school counselor, school psychologist, or principal. Teachers refer students to any other responsible adult, hoping for change. The teacher's behaviors express a bankruptcy of effective ideas with students on disciplinary matters. This referral has an explicit "fix the child" message which counselors, psychologists, or principals may be unable to achieve.

Teachers may express the following faulty beliefs when referring students:

1. the child is the problem;

2. the parent, counselor, psychologist, or principal can fix the problem; and

3. the teacher has no (or a limited) part in this repair process.

When teachers ignore their part in the disciplinary process, they also ignore part of the child when dealing with academic achievement.

Teacher Beliefs

The influence of the teacher's beliefs about self and the students cannot be overemphasized. If a student is in a classroom, the influences of the teacher's beliefs are inescapable. Consider the following example:

Janice began the second grade in Mr. Bowman's classroom with new clothes, pencils, and an eagerness to learn. However, Janice's older brother, now in the fourth grade, also had been in Mr. Bowman's class. He was a bright and capable child, able to keep up with all work.

One month into the school year, Janice was having trouble in her reading group. She was struggling with certain concepts and was becoming discouraged. Mr. Bowman said to Janice, *"I'm sure you'll do well, because your brother was one of my best students."*

What does Janice conclude from Mr. Bowman's remarks? What does Mr. Bowman believe about her? Was this encouraging or discouraging? The intentions were good but the method did not achieve the desired result.

Understanding teacher beliefs is essential. We must understand that each teacher has a set of beliefs which is the basis for behaviors in the classroom. Some of the beliefs are effective, enhancing the teacher/student relationship and the ability of the students to grow and learn. Other beliefs are detrimental, causing relationship problems with students. We can examine some of the common faulty beliefs of teachers, so that we can recognize their implications for the consultation relationship. The common faulty teacher beliefs have been presented in Dinkmeyer, McKay, and Dinkmeyer (1980):

1. **Students must cooperate with me.**

   Implication: I am in charge; students will do what I say. If they do not, I am not an effective disciplinarian. Cooperation is based on my terms and means compliance with my needs.

2. **I must be capable of handling all students and all situations, or I am not a good teacher.**

   Implication: I must handle all students with the skills I now have. I have learned everything about handling students. A consultation relationship is an indication of failure.

3. *My plans must succeed at all costs.*

Implication: My plan is the only one; no room exists for give and take in the relationship. To be in control or to "win" in challenges with my students is important. I have little flexibility in my relationships with others.

4. *Some students are naturally bad and must be punished when they fail to cooperate.*

Implication: Not all students are good; some have no hope of correction. My approach is to use punishment as the discipline system to create compliance. The only discipline system which is effective is based on controls from outside the child.

5. *I must control the classroom and all students so they do not control me. To be out of control is dangerous.*

Implication: To be in control is important. This concern is based on a real issue: how do I effectively handle a room of 30 or more students? However, recognize that many teachers have not had extensive training in classroom management techniques. Others have been taught discipline systems which emphasize control as the primary technique.

6. *Unhappiness is externally caused, and I have no ability to control or influence my feelings.*

Implication: I cannot expect to change the present situation. For me to change has no "payoff." There are no resources to help me change.

7. *Children are the product of their heredity and the larger environment, and cannot be changed.*

Implication: The student cannot be influenced by any of my actions or beliefs. The influence of the school is minimal.

Teachers will frequently present one or more of these beliefs to the consultant. A teacher is unlikely to say, "*I must be in control,*" but their actions and words will be consistent with this belief. See Figure 5.1 for a summary of how beliefs affect a teacher's behavior.

(Continued on page 134)

Ineffective   Characteristics

Teacher's Belief	Teacher's Behavior	Results for Students
I must control.	Demands obedience. Rewards and punishes. Tries to win. Insists is right and students wrong. Overprotects.	Rebel; must win or be right. Hide true feelings. Seek revenge. Feel life is unfair. Give up. Evade, lie, steal. Lack self-discipline.
I am superior.	Pities students. Takes resposibility. Overprotects. Acts self-righteous. Shames students.	Learn to pity selves and blame others. Criticize others. Feel life is unfair. Feel inadequate. Become dependent. Feel need to be superior.
I am entitled. You owe me.	Is overconcerned with fairness. Gives with strings attached.	Don't trust others. Feel life is unfair. Feel exploited. Learn to exploit others.
I must be perfect.	Demands perfection from all. Finds fault. Is overconcerned about what others think. Pushes students to make self look good.	Believe they are never good enough. Become perfectionists. Feel discouraged. Worry about others' opinions.
I don't count. Others are more important than I.	Is permissive. Sets no guidelines. Gives in to students' demands. Feels guilty about saying no.	Expect to get own way. Are confused. Do not respect rights of others. Are selfish.

Figure 5.1. Ineffective and effective characteristics of teachers. From *Systematic Training for Effective Teaching* (STET): *Teacher's Handbook* by Dinkmeyer, McKay, and Dinkmeyer, 1980, American Guidance Service, Inc., Circle Pines, MN 55014-1796. Reproduced with permission.

Figure 5.1. continued.

Effective Characteristics

Teacher's Belief	Teacher's Behavior	Results for Students
I believe students can make decisions.	Permits choices. Encourages.	Feel self-confident. Try. Contribute. Solve problems. Become resourceful.
I am equal, not more or less than others.	Believes in and respects students. Encourages independence. Gives choices and responsiblity. Expects students to contribute.	Develop self-reliance, independence, responsibility. Learn to make decisions. Respect selves and others. Believe in equality.
I believe in mutual respect.	Promotes equality. Encourages mutual respect. Avoids promoting guilt feelings.	Respect selves and others. Have increased social interest. Trust others.
I am human: I have the "courage to be imperfect."	Sets realistic standards. Focuses on strengths. Encourages. Is not concerned with own image. Is patient.	Focus on task at hand, not on self-elevation. See mistakes as challenge. Have courage to try new experiences. Are tolerant of others.
I believe all people are important, including myself.	Encourages mutual respect. Invites contributions. Refuses to be "doormat." Knows when to set limits and say no.	Know and accept limits. Respect rights of others.

The role of the consultant is to listen carefully to all consultee statements for the underlying beliefs. Recognize that teachers often begin by focusing on changing the student. While listening is important, this is not the place to begin the consultation relationship. Certain procedures must be utilized to stimulate recognition of beliefs, to offer alternative beliefs and behaviors, and to create an atmosphere conducive to this recognition, presentation, and change.

INDIVIDUAL CONSULTATION

Teachers frequently present requests on an individual basis. Rarely do two or more teachers approach the consultant about a similar situation. Each request often focuses on one student.

The consultant therefore may see a need to work with teachers on a one to one basis. Individual teacher consultation can be hampered by several considerations:

1. ***Advice-giving seems an immediate, if not natural response.*** The tendency is for consultants to hear feelings, beliefs, and explore alternatives with students. But with teachers, we give advice. The answer-machine approach, hoping to produce simple solutions by prescription, often ignores the feelings, beliefs, and alternatives for each teacher. The consultant as merely an advice-giver is an outdated, ineffective professional resource.

2. ***One cannot consult effectively unless the internal frame of reference of the consultee is understood.*** It is vital that the perceptions and beliefs be identified and examined. In an individual consultation relationship, this examination is limited by the consultee's willingness to expose these beliefs with the individual consultant.

3. ***Individual consultation presents opportunities for the teacher to respond to ideas*** with comments such as "*That*

doesn't work," *"I've already tried that,"* or *"When were you last in a classroom?!"* Consultant suggestions may be blocked when the teacher has no peers offering feedback.

4. **Consultants are limited to their own resources—their education, experiences, and ideas.** These limited resources never embrace all types of situations which teachers will present. If the teacher is in a group of peers, the disadvantages of the consultant's expertise can be minimized.

A rationale for working with teachers in groups is therefore established. Unless one is aware of the potential benefits of didactic-experiential group, consultation with teachers can be a discouraging, limited experience.

Therefore, teacher groups can be established for both problem solving and educational purposes. Teacher education course work does not completely prepare individuals for the classroom. Perhaps less than one-third of those receiving teacher certification have any course work in groups. If a teacher is not aware of group forces, dynamics, and opportunities to influence groups, a basic part of the educational process for our educators is missing. Failing to cover basic concepts such as group dynamics undereducates our teachers.

TEACHER EDUCATION IN-SERVICE COMPONENTS

Teacher in-service training must go beyond the single day in August that includes outside speakers or time provided for organizing the classroom. The skills needed by teachers require a consistent approach to acquiring these skills throughout the year. A number of teacher study groups have emerged around Adlerian texts. Among the books that are useful in applying the

Adlerian approach to the classroom are Albert (1989), Baruth and Eckstein (1982), Carlson and Thorpe (1984), Dinkmeyer and Dreikurs (1963), Glenn and Nelsen (1987), and Painter and Corsini (1990).

A more comprehensive approach to teacher in-service involves the use of *Systematic Training for Effective Teaching* (STET) (Dinkmeyer, McKay, & Dinkmeyer, 1980). STET topics include understanding behavior and misbehavior, understanding yourself as a teacher, encouragement, communication and listening, expressing your ideas and feelings to students, exploring alternatives and problem solving discussion, promoting responsible behavior through natural and logical consequences, applying natural and logical consequences, understanding the group, group leadership skills, group guidance, group class meetings, understanding and dealing with special problems, and working with parents. The STET program can be taught in a comparatively short one hour per session format or a more thorough two hour format. The two hour format contains the following elements:

1. A group building activity. This helps participants become better acquainted with each other, become more cohesive as a group, and learn how to apply these concepts in their classrooms.

2. Discussion of the previous week's activity assignment. In each session members of the workshop are asked to carry out during the ensuing week an activity assignment applying the concepts learned. This presents an opportunity to get feedback on how one's beliefs and skills mesh in teaching.

3. Discussion of assigned reading. The STET program has an extensive teacher's handbook which provides stimulation for discussions regarding the application of these concepts to the classrooms.

4. Skill building exercises. The STET program contains cassette tapes setting forth situations in which teachers are asked to respond to challenges, misbehavior, and

difficult situations by listening to recorded interactions with students. These exercises provide an excellent opportunity for responding to real-life situations.

5. An opportunity to respond to problem situations. This can be done by role-playing and reacting or by written response to the situation followed by discussion.

6. Points to remember. This is a list of the basic principles taught in each session. They are discussed and reviewed.

7. Problem situations. These provide another opportunity to experience the major concepts and the skill that is called for in each problem situation.

8. Summary. Summarizing is an essential part of the program. It enables members of the group to identify and clarify what they have learned and to give the leaders some indication of what the members are taking from the session.

The one hour session can best be accomplished by

1. discussing the previous week's activity assignment,

2. discussing the assigned reading,

3. using the exercises, and

4. summarizing.

The STET approach divides each session into a learning cycle with three major components. In the first part, new ideas are presented through the reading and charts. These ideas become skills which are practiced in the teacher group through audio incidents and written problem situations. The third part is applications; ways to use the ideas with students.

STET is based upon the importance of applying the democratic process to the educational experience and must be taught in a manner that models the principles and procedures it advocates.

ESSENTIAL TOPICS FOR IN-SERVICE PROGRAM

We feel that an effective program needs to include the following six topics. Each topic is followed by explanation.

A Useful, Pragmatic Theory of Human Behavior

How does the student operate in the classroom? Many teachers do not have an effective understanding of themselves and their students. The result is often confusion.

Human behavior is usually predictable. In Chapter 3, the Adlerian approach to human behavior showed teachers a better understanding of the students in the classroom. In particular, the four goals of misbehavior are an illuminating concept. It allows teachers to understand accurately and to react to students.

An equally important aspect of human behavior is understanding ourselves. In the consultation relationship, this information is difficult if not impossible to present in a one-to-one setting. Instead, information on human behavior and self-understanding stands a greater chance of acceptance when presented in a group and educational setting.

Motivation Techniques

Many students who require the most motivation do not receive any, and those requiring the least receive the most motivation. When a praise and reward system is created, the least motivated are left behind. Additional motivation techniques such as encouragement can be taught and practiced in the group.

Communication Skills

Few people are naturally good listeners. How can we listen to students?

Traditional teacher roles may not recognize the importance of listening to students as a motivation skill. When students are heard, they are more motivated. Essential communication skills for teachers include reflective listening, I-messages, and problem-solving conferences. The consultant models these skills while working with the teacher.

Discipline Techniques

Discipline often focuses on techniques for regaining control in the classroom. Effective discipline procedures are preventive. Time-outs and referrals to principals or counselors are not a total, effective discipline system.

Most teachers are familiar with punishment-based discipline systems. A system based on natural and logical consequences is an alternative. Each choice for the student is a learning process. Even if the "wrong" behavior occurs, the student learns from this choice.

Working with Groups

Teachers receive little or no education in group dynamics. Group dynamics explain the individual goals of misbehavior. All students *always* seek to belong within the group: An individual's goals of misbehavior, and appropriate behavior, occur within the group setting and dynamics.

The group context of behavior and misbehavior, group dynamics, group leadership skills, classroom group guidance, and classroom meetings are essential teaching skills. Because teachers may have no previous education in these group areas, consultation education might begin with any of these principles.

Working with Parents

Effective consultation procedure with parents are fully discussed in Chapter 7. Perhaps the most rapid shift within our society is occurring within the family. Fewer than one-half the children born today will grow up within an "intact" (two continuously married parents) family.

The consultant cannot ignore the parents, nor can we neglect the opportunity to teach teachers how to deal with parents.

RATIONALE FOR PROBLEM-SOLVING GROUPS

Working with teachers in education groups helps the consultation process. Teachers have a new core of information, skills, and self-awareness. These assets are efficiently transmitted in education groups. Once teachers acquire this baseline, consultation for problem-solving can begin.

Working with teachers in groups is more meaningful when the consultant recognizes that we are indivisible, social, decision-making beings whose actions have a social purpose. This view of teachers and students as social beings develops new awareness and gives meaning to all verbal and nonverbal interactions. It is a comprehensive understanding of human thought and behavior.

In a group, teachers can become more aware of their traditional methods of responding to difficult children. The group setting provides a new way to see the life-style, faulty assumptions, and mistaken ideas of both student and teacher. It is essentially a holistic approach. The group setting takes into consideration not only the intellect, feelings, and behavior of the child, but also the teacher.

Groups create experiences for teachers in a supporting, caring, accepting atmosphere. The teacher has access to feedback about personal behavior, feelings, and attitudes, and through this, can develop a new perspective on relationships. Effective procedures for working with children can be discussed. The group also benefits teachers who do not have difficulties with children. It gives them an opportunity to contribute to each other.

In order to understand group dynamics, teachers must experience being a group member. Often teacher education has not permitted them to have an experience either as a group member or a group leader. If we are going to deal with the whole child, we must engage teachers by participation as "whole teachers."

Placing teachers in a group recognizes that most problems are interpersonal and social. The challenge that the teacher presents originated in a group interaction with the student. The teacher can become aware of the necessity of understanding behavior in its social context. The teacher group then has the opportunity to analyze the student's life-style. The student's unique approach to the tasks of life will be consistent with the self-concept and assumptions about life. More important, the consultant and the group have an opportunity to observe the teacher's life-style and the characteristic responses to students and members of the group.

The group setting provides the consultant and group members with an extremely valuable social laboratory. It is a miniature society or micro-community which reflects the school's atmosphere. As the teacher learns to function as a member of the group, insights can be developed as to how the student functions in a group. Through this process, teachers also are able to understand how they function in a group. The group has diagnostic, educational, and therapeutic values.

Behaviors can be observed in the group setting. Teachers cannot mask or bluff their way through a group of peers. The teacher's characteristic approach to working on problems is shared in the group setting.

A number of therapeutic effects can be processed in the group setting. The group provides the opportunity for a unique type of acceptance. This is a setting in which teachers can experience the empathy which comes from their peers. It also provides the opportunity to ventilate and express how they feel.

In the group, teachers try out ideas and process the feedback from other teachers in the group. Teachers recognize that problems with children are universal; other teachers are experiencing the same challenges. Universalization can help the group build trust, cooperation, and momentum. This can stimulate one's altruism and desire to help fellow professionals become more effective. Each member helps every other member.

The group provides teachers with an opportunity to hear other challenges and develop some ideas about how to handle a situation which, to this point, they have not even encountered. **Spectator therapy**, learning from another's experience, is a major benefit.

THE C GROUP

C groups are concerned with three professional roles within the school—the counselor, the administrator, and teachers. Few teacher education programs or traditional school in-services are similar to the C group. Components of the C group are

consultation,
collaboration,
communication,
clarification,
change, and
commitment.

The group is both didactic (teaching new skills) and experiential (sharing feelings). The content comes from sharing concerns and the process involves analysis of the purpose of behavior, identification of assets, and contracts for change.

Consultants need to thoroughly understand the purpose and the value of working with teachers in C groups.

For example, many counselors are receiving numerous teacher-referred students as discipline problems. Teacher groups can reduce the pressure to "fix and return" these students because sharing problem-solving skills with teachers will lead to reduction in the number of student referrals for discipline.

Most classroom behavior problems are interpersonal in nature. Students represent one-half of the teacher-student relationship. This emphasizes the need to work with teachers—the adult one-half of the relationship.

By stimulating positive interaction among teachers and between the counselor and teachers, each C group indirectly reaches hundreds of children.

Although counseling and psychological services to students and other elements within the school have their own value, teacher groups often are the only direct and tangible evidence of these services to teachers.

The consultant can use this rationale to enthusiastically communicate to administrators and the teaching staff the value of consultant directed teacher groups.

Administrative support of the group is essential. Principals should be aware of the purpose and merit of the group and encourage participation from staff. The educational and voluntary nature of the C group should be emphasized. From the administration standpoint, C groups can provide an effective training experience in reducing classroom behavior problems. They increase teachers' disciplinary effectiveness. The C group also stresses related elements of effective teaching, such as how to motivate and encourage students.

Teachers themselves need to be fully apprised of the nature of the group. C groups and similar teacher services can be misunderstood and perceived as therapy or an indication of ineffective teaching. They actually represent an extremely valuable laboratory for education, sharing of experiences, and resolving of common classroom challenges.

ORGANIZING THE C GROUP

Each C group consists of four to six teachers who meet one hour each week for a minimum of six to eight weeks. Groups often meet before school, at mutual noon hours, or during the planning periods, both during and after school.

Administrative support is necessary to approve the time and space needed, along with appropriate changes in schedules and responsibilities. The C group is not a sensitivity group nor is it an administrative-backed prescription to cure the school's "worst" teachers. The first group contains a cross-section of the staff including those who have social and professional power within the school.

A demonstration and brief explanation at a staff meeting can be the first stimulation of interest. Deliberate development of teacher interest and knowledge of the C group is essential. At this meeting or whenever groups are formed, each member must make a commitment to attend all group meetings. Teachers should not join a C group after the first meeting. Instead, their interest can be the basis of forming the next C group.

A C group should be a heterogenous blend of experience, orientations, and skills. The common denominator is the age of the students each teacher represents, because behavior problems are often similar at certain age and grade levels. A group of fourth grade teachers, for example, more easily identifies with the classrooms involved than does a group of first and fifth grade teachers. Nevertheless, primary, intermediate, and junior high teachers can be of assistance to each other.

C groups begin with the consultant's presentation of an Adlerian theory of behavior and misbehavior. Each group member must understand these principles of misbehavior and goal identification. The four goals of misbehavior (attention, power, revenge, and display of inadequacy) and subsequent teacher actions in response to these misbehaviors are the foundation of the group's knowledge. This allows each teacher in the group to have a common base from which to understand student behavior and misbehavior.

Once the group has this common knowledge of behavior, solving misbehavior problems is a focus of the group. Each week, time is allotted to teachers for presentation of a student behavior problem.

The C group offers the following:

- A theory of human behavior that speaks directly to classroom misbehavior.

- A technique for identifying student misbehavior goals.

- A realization by teachers that goal identification is based on their reactions and feelings about misbehavior, e.g., a specific reaction such as annoyance indicates a specific misbehavior goal (attention). In this systematic and lawful understanding of human behavior, "answers" are available to every teacher who comes to recognize the purpose of misbehavior.

- Suggestions for teachers' reactions to misbehavior that do not inadvertently "feed" the misbehavior's purpose. Many initial or conventional responses to student misbehavior suffer from this unintentional dynamic. For example, a show of force or punishment in response to power-oriented misbehavior only impresses and reinforces the student(s) belief in the importance of power. Paying attention to attention-getting misbehavior meets the goal (attention) of that misbehavior.

- A procedure whereby teachers can share misbehavior incidents within a group to identify the goal and corrective actions.

- A realization that teacher-student conflict presents an opportunity for teachers to change when teachers often have assumed previously that their verbal commands produce such change in students.

The consultant's leadership in the C group begins with an effective presentation of the curriculum and then structures the group into a problem-solving and follow-through procedure. Each group member is the focus for approximately ten to fifteen minutes. A specific incident and anecdotes are presented and worked on by the group. The leader is not an expert to which these problems are referred. Group members work with each other and the leader encourages this interaction throughout the group sessions. The teachers thus develop problem-solving skills and the ability to consult with one another specifically and effectively.

This approach has been labeled the C group because factors which make it effective begin with the letter "C."

Collaboration. The group collaborates and works together on mutual concerns. The leader has an equal position. No superior/inferior relationships exist between the leader and the group or between members of the group. They are in the group for the purpose of mutual help.

Consultation. Consultation is both received and provided by the teachers. The interaction that occurs within the group between the leader and the members helps group members to become aware of new approaches with students.

Clarification. The group clarifies for each member their belief systems, their feelings, and the congruency or incongruousness between their behavior, beliefs, and feelings.

Confrontation. Confrontation makes the group more productive in so far as it produces more realistic and honest feedback. The expectation is that each individual will see himself or herself, his or her purposes, attitudes, and beliefs, and will be willing to confront other members about their psychological make-up. Members in the group confront each other because they want to help each member to become more effective.

Concern. The group is concerned and shows that it cares. This concern leads members to collaborate, consult, clarify, and confront in order to develop the human potential of both students and group members.

Confidentiality. The group is confidential in the sense that whatever is discussed within the group stays within the group. The purpose is to be mutually helpful, not to generate gossip.

Commitment to Change. The group helps individuals to develop a commitment to change. Participants in the group become involved in helping members to recognize that they really can change only themselves. They may come to the group expecting to change students, but they soon learn that they must develop a specific commitment to take action before the next C group that will attempt to change their approach to the problem.

Channel for Communication. The group is a new channel for communication in so far as it communicates not only ideas but feelings, attitudes, and beliefs. Members become involved with each other as persons.

Change Behavior. The group members recognize that changing students' behavior often requires that they change their beliefs, attitudes, and procedures.

Cohesion. The group is most effective when there is cohesion and the members work together as a team.

C GROUP IN ACTION

The problem-solving nature of C group is demonstrated in the following excerpt from the second session of a C group.

Consultant: *Let's apply our knowledge of misbehavior to a specific student. Does anyone have a misbehavior incident they'd like to work on?*

Mrs. Jones: *OK. Let's really try this with one of my kids, Rick. Everyone has problems with his clowning around.*

Consultant: *What's something that happened between you and Rick?*

Mrs. Jones: *He usually disrupts quiet work periods until I move him to the back of the room away from others.*

Consultant: *Could you give me a specific example of this so we can work it through the four questions for goal identification:*

1. *What did the student do?*

2. *How did the teacher respond to the misbehavior?*

3. *How did the teacher feel when the misbehavior was occurring?*

4. *How did the student respond to the teacher's corrective actions?*

(This is the procedure for sharing anecdotes in the group. Teachers refer to the chart on Goals of Misbehavior throughout the C Group session as they apply the four questions to their anecdotes.)

Mrs. Jones: *OK. Today Rick wouldn't keep quiet during individual reading. He loudly tapped his pencil and tried to talk to others.*

Consultant: *What did you do?*

Mrs. Jones: *I told him to stop at once and then a second time I told him he'd have to go to the back table to work if he couldn't leave us alone. He didn't, and the third time I told him to go to the back table. He settled down and that was the end of it for that period.*

Consultant: *OK. We know the first, second, and fourth parts. What about your feelings? That really helps us identify the goals of Rick's misbehavior. Different goals produce different feelings in us.*

Mrs. Jones: *I didn't really feel angry or hurt. It was just an annoyance. That was the feeling. Would that mean attention-getting misbehavior?*

Consultant: *What do others think?*

Mr. Effenheim: *It does seem that Rick's goal of attention was met. He got it three times from you in a very short time.*

Mrs. Jones: *I did pay attention to his antics. He does like to annoy me—it seems that that's all we do some days.*

Consultant: *What can you do differently when Rick does this?*

Mrs. Jones: *If his purpose is to get my attention, I'd have to ignore him and recognize his need for attention on my own terms—by paying attention to his positive behaviors—when he's not making a bid for it in an unpleasant way.*

Mr. Effenheim: *That seems hard to do. Can you just ignore him?*

Mrs. Jones: *You mean let it go and see if he stops? I could, but what if he continues?*

Consultant: *If our guess about Rick is right, ignoring him denies the "payoff" he is getting now. He'd see you are not interested in what he is doing. When you do say something, you are meeting the goal of the misbehavior and in effect saying "I am interested" when you think your words convey "I'm not interested."*

Miss Howell: *So with attention-getting misbehavior, even saying "stop it" pays attention!* (group laughs)

Consultant: *Yes. Often our initial response to misbehaviors is exactly the opposite of what we want.*

Mrs. Jones: *OK. I'll ignore him and see if it stops.*

Mr. Effenheim: *It seems you can't be halfway. You really need to turn off to him. He probably won't stop it the first time.*

Mrs. Jones: *That will really be difficult, but I do see how it's something I can do. Telling him to stop doesn't work, so I'll stop that. How long will this take, do you think?*

Mr. Effenheim: *It's probably like breaking a bad habit for both you and Rick.*

Consultant: *Can you ignore him this week and tell us about your progress when we meet next time?*

Mrs. Jones: *Yes, I will.*

The conclusion to this scenario is vital to effective C groups. Teachers must commit to change and recognize that a "once or twice" attitude produces few changes. The group is a uniquely effective method of encouraging new procedures by teachers with peer acceptance to test new behaviors and the opportunity to learn from others. Once the C group establishes an understanding of misbehavior and the anecdote procedure for identifying goals, the leader allocates time for all group members to present their anecdotes.

The group atmosphere is one of commitment to applying new ideas during the week and sharing these at the next meeting. A powerfully persuasive encouragement to change occurs when a teacher reports successes to the group. The group allows the opportunity to learn by others' experiences and to be encouraged by them.

In summary, the C group recognizes that every student misbehavior is interpersonal and presents an opportunity for teachers to change the interaction between students and themselves. Instead of working with the student, C groups utilize the skills and abilities of the teacher to produce change.

THE ENCOURAGEMENT PROCESS

In the day-to-day activities of the classroom, the encouragement process can be a very effective means of reinforcement (Dinkmeyer & Dreikurs, 1963; Dinkmeyer & Losoncy, 1980). Consultants model the encouragement process in direct work with teachers as well as teach these important concepts. Through careful planning and organization, the teacher then can use the encouragement process to help pupils.

The process of encouragement specifically involves:

- Valuing individuals as he is, not as his reputation indicates nor as you hope he will be—but as they are.
- Showing faith in the individual. This will help the individual to develop a feeling of "can-ness" or a belief in self.
- Having faith in the child's ability. This enables the teacher to win the child's confidence while building the individual's self-respect.
- Giving recognition for effort as well as a job well done.
- Using the group to help the child develop.
- Integrating the group so that the individual child can discover his or her place.
- Planning for success, assisting in the development of skills.
- Identifying and focusing on strengths and assets rather than mistakes.
- Using the individual's interests in order to motivate instruction.
(Dinkmeyer & Dreikurs, 1963)

Encouragement is a process, not a single effort. It lets students know that the teacher believes in them and will treat them with respect and trust. The individual's value as a person is reflected in the teacher's attitude toward the student and the student's behaviors.

Encouragement should not be confused with praise, although the two are both efforts to motivate students. Praise puts the emphasis upon the product, while encouragement stresses the effort of contribution. (See Figure 5.2)

Dinkmeyer, McKay, and Dinkmeyer (1980) outline the differences between praise and encouragement:

Encouragement is helping students believe in themselves and in their abilities.

- Encouragement is a basic attitude toward yourself and other people.

- Encouragement is different from praise. Praise goes to those who excel or come in first; encouragement can be given for any positive movement. Encouragement does not have to be earned.

The differences between praise and encouragement are sometimes subtle. A teacher once described the differences between the two as follows: *"Imagine your students are running a race. The cheering, prizes, and applause at the finish line are praise. Encouragement is what you do during the race."*

Praise affects the child's self-image. The impression that personal worth depends upon how measuring up to the demands

(Continued on page 155)

PRAISE

Underlying Characteristics to Child	Message Sent to Child	Possible Results
Focus is on external control.	"You are worthwhile only when you do what I want." "You cannot and should not be trusted."	Child learns to measure worth by ability to conform; or child rebels (views any form of cooperation as giving in).
Focus is on external evaluation.	"To be worthwhile, you must please me." "Please me or perish."	Child learns to measure worth on how well she pleases others. Child learns to fear disapproval.
Rewards come only for well done, completed tasks.	"To be worthwhile, you must meet my standards."	Child develops unrealistic standards and learns to measure worth by how closely she reaches perfection. Child learns to dread failure.
Focuses on self-evaluation and personal gain.	"You're the best. You must remain superior to others to be wortwhile."	Child learns to be overcompetitive, to get ahead at the expense of others. Feels worthwhile only when "on top."

ENCOURAGEMENT

Underlying Characteristics	Message Sent to Child	Possible Results
Focus is on child's ability to manage life constructively.	"I trust you to become responsible and independent."	Child learns courage to be imperfect and willingness to try. Child gains self-confidence and comes to feel responsible for own behavior.
Focus is on internal evaluation.	"How you feel about yourself and your own efforts is most important."	Child learns to evalutate own progress and to make own decisions.
Recognizes effort and improvement.	"You don't have to be perfect. Effort and improvement are important."	Child learns to value efforts of self and others. Child develops desire to stay with tasks (persistence).
Focuses on assets, contributions, and appreciation.	"Your contribution counts. We function better with you. We appreciate what you have done."	Child learns to use talents and efforts for good of all, not only for personal gain. Child learns to feel glad for successes of others as well as own successess.

Figure 5.2. Differences between praise and encouragement. From *The Growing Teacher*, by Carlson and Thorpe (1984). Englewood Cliffs, NJ: Prentice-Hall, Inc. (p.39–40). Reprinted by permission.

and values of others comes with praise. *"If I am praised, my personal worth is high. If I am scolded, I am worthless."* The ability to cope with challenges cannot depend on the opinions (positive or negative) of others.

Students may come to see praise as a right. Therefore, life is unfair if praise isn't received for every effort: *"Poor me—no one appreciates me."* Students may feel no obligation to perform if no praise is received. *"What's in it for me? What will I get out of it? If no praise (reward) is forthcoming, why should I bother?"* These students may be some of the highest achievers in the classroom. They are "hooked on praise." Praise can be discouraging. If the student is not "praise-worthy," what can the teacher say to the student?

If a student has set high standards, praise may sound insincere. This is particularly true when efforts fail to measure up to personal standards. In such a student, praise only serves to increase anger and resentment at others for not understanding the disappointment.

In order to feel adequate, students must feel useful and know that their contributions count. Since motivation to learn and change manifests itself in terms of how people see themselves, those who teach and consult must become instruments of positive feedback. We can help teachers and students feel useful by identifying their talents and suggesting ways in which they might use these talents to make a contribution. A list of positive talents is included in Figure 5.3.

We help teachers and students believe in themselves by believing in them. We must communicate confidence and play down mistakes. We must be sensitive and alert to point out positive aspects of their efforts, recognizing improvement as well as final accomplishments.

friendly	aware	popular
highly regarded	anticipating	peaceful
thoughtful	strong	appealing
affectionate	sensitive	determined
well-liked	alert	sure
adored	keen	attractive
kind	content	untroubled
alive	comfortable	graceful
independent	relaxed	enthusiastic
capable	at ease	eager
happy	wide awake	optimistic
proud	worthy	joyful
gratified	admired	courageous
excited	sympathetic	hopeful
good	concerned	pleased
inspired	appreciated	excited
jolly	secure	interested
warm	glad	turned-on
daring	brave	intelligent

Figure 5.3. List of positive talents that could be recognized and encouraged.

HOW TO ENCOURAGE

The following points will be helpful in the encouragement process and motivating teachers and students:

- Build on teachers' and students' strong points. Look for positive efforts as well as results.

- Minimize the teachers' or students' weak points. Avoid nagging, criticizing, or spending an undue amount of time talking about what could have been done.

- Tell teachers and students what you appreciate. Some encouraging statements could be *"I really enjoy seeing you smile"* or *"I like the neatness of your paper. It's such a pleasure to read" or "Thank you for turning in your assignment early. Now I have more time to spend on reading it before the avalanche of other papers hits."*

- Be friendly. Take time to listen and show care and concern.

- Demonstrate your appreciation for the teacher or student. Such things as a personal comment, a special note, or an arm around the shoulder convey liking in a meaningful way. Spending time with students and teachers during and after class or after school hours also shows that you care.

- Suggest small steps in doing a task. The entire job may seem too overwhelming. Give discouraged teachers or students a small amount of work to do. As they finish each increment, they will feel encouraged.

- Be humorous. A wink, a pun, or a laugh at oneself can warm relationships. Always laugh with teachers and students, never at them.

- Recognize effort. Recognize attempts to do a task even though a job might not be well done. In initial stages of a new behavior or learning task, teachers and students need extra support and encouragement. Once they develop proficiency and begin to experience success, the secondary reinforcing property of the act itself takes over.

- Become aware of the interaction between yourself and the student or teacher. Realize that all behavior has a purpose and that often our responses are counterproductive. For example, when a student annoys us in an effort to gain our attention, we usually respond with a lecture on inappropriate behavior, scold, punish, or give some other form of attention. This attention actually supports the negative behavior rather than eliminates it.

- Discipline students with fewer words. Actions are more effective than words. Angry words are discouraging and often untrue. After taking firm action, resume talking with the student in a friendly manner, conveying the impression that you still and always will respect the student as important. The behavior is what is not acceptable.

• Do not own the teachers' or students' problems. Allow teachers or students to solve their own problems. This indicates your faith in them, giving them flexibility in tending to their own concerns and interests.

• Do not use rewards and punishments. These procedures are discouraging and ineffective.

• Accept teachers and students as they are, not as you wish them to be.

• Be understanding and empathetic. Look at the world from the teacher's or student's point of view.

THREE-STEP METHOD OF ENCOURAGEMENT

Step 1: Identify Positive Behaviors, Traits, and Efforts.

Many educators have a difficult time identifying positive behavior. Figure 5.4 offers some examples of positive behavior, along with the associated mental health principles.

In order to motivate students, we must have a clear idea of what we would like to encourage and what we would like to see changed. We must indicate what this means in terms of behavior, including the required effort and movement.

Sometimes we think we are being helpful and guiding students in positive ways when in reality we are not. Discouraging statements made *prior to* behavior include the following:

Don't get dirty.
Watch yourself.
You aren't old enough.
Be careful.
Let me do it for you.
Let me show you how.
I know you can't do it.
If younger children can do it, so can you.
Look at how well Susie does it.

Discouraging statements made *after* the behavior include the following:

No, that's not right.
I shouldn't have trusted you.
You could have done better.
I've told you a thousand times.
When will you become responsible?
If you'd only listened to me.
If only you weren't so lazy.
You did it again.
Oh, when will you learn?
Don't you have any pride in your work?

The following list will be helpful in identifying personality strengths in students.

Special Aptitudes: Intuition. Making guesses that usually turn out right. Having a "green thumb." Mechanical or sales

(Continued on page 162)

Principle	Behaviors
Respects the rights of others.	Takes turns.
	Does not monopolize everyone's time .
	Cleans up supplies after an art lesson.
	Does not disturb other students who are working or concentrating on something.
Is tolerant of others.	Walks slowly so others can keep up.
	Waits quietly while others complete their assignments or tasks.
	Accepts all children and all abilities on the playground.
	Helps students from other cultures with English or comprehending school rules.
Is interested in others.	Includes/ invites others to play.
	Shows concern for absent students.
	Volunteers to help others.
	Talks to and socializes with other students.
	Promotes or suggests social functions.
Cooperates with others.	Completes assignments on time.
	Works facilitatively in groups.
	Listens to what others say.
	Works with others rather than against them.
Encourages others.	Notices and acknowledges positive change and good performance in others.
	Focuses on positive aspects of other students.
	Acts optimistic.
	Gives all students a chance when playing games.
Is courageous.	Takes risks.
	Enjoys novel and different experiences.
	Is calm under pressure of tests.
	Acts enthusiastically toward challenges.

Figure 5.4. Positive mental health. From *The Growing Teacher* by Carlson and Thorpe (1984) pp. 34-5. Reproduced with permission.

Figure 5.4 continued.

Has a true sense of self-worth.	Likes and validates himself. Acts in a realistic fashion. Understands and accepts his assets and liabilities. Has the courage to be imperfect.
Has a feeling of belonging.	Frequently mentions groups to which he belongs (e.g., friends, Scouts, sports teams, church clubs). Feels accepted in school and does not need to act out to find his place. Makes a positive contribution to a group. Exercises a vote/voice in appropriate activities and procedures.
Has socially acceptable goals.	Works within school rules. Is involved in the classroom. Cooperates with others and is just and fair. Doesn't precipitate fights and withdraws from physical conflict.
Puts forth genuine effort.	Tries hard on assignments. Does homework. Participates in discussions. Becomes absorbed and interested in learning.
Meets the needs of the situation.	Makes good decisions. Is able to solve problems. Handles spontaneous situations in a responsible manner. Does not under- or over-react to assignments.
Is willing to share rather han thinking, "How much can I get?"	Readily offers assistance to others. Shares lunch, pencils, crayons, etc. More process-oriented than outcome-oriented.
Thinks of "we" rather than just "I."	Uses words like "we," "us," and "our" rather than just "I," "me," and "mine." Shows caring and concern for others. Frequently offers to share.

ability. Skill in construction or repairing things. Mathematical ability.

Intellectual Strengths: Applying reasoning ability to problem solving. intellectual curiosity. Thinking out ideas and expressing them orally or in writing. Openness to accepting new ideas. Original or creative thinking. The ability to enjoy learning.

Education and Training: Any high grades. Improvement in grades. Scholastic honors. Vocational training or self-education through study and organized reading.

Work: Experience in a particular line of work. Job satisfaction, including enjoying one's work, getting along with co-workers, taking pride in job duties.

Aesthetic Strengths: Recognizing and appreciating beauty in nature and the arts.

Organizational Strengths: Demonstrating leadership abilities. Developing and planning short- and long-range goals. Ability in giving orders as well as in carrying them out.

Hobbies and Crafts: Special interests and training in hobbies and crafts.

Expressive Arts: Dancing, writing, sketching, painting, sculpture, modeling with clay. Ability to improvise music or to play a musical instrument. Rhythmic ability.

Health: Good health represents a strength. Emphasis on maintaining or improving health through nutrition, exercise, and stress management.

Sports and Outdoor Activities: Active participation in outdoor activities and organized sports, camping, or hunting.

Imaginative and Creative Strengths: Using creativity and imagination for new and different ideas.

Relationship Strengths: Ability to meet people easily and make them feel comfortable. Ability to communicate with strangers. Treating others with consideration, politeness, and respect. Being aware of the needs and feelings of others. Listening to what people are saying. Helping others to be aware of their strengths and abilities.

Emotional Strengths: Ability to give and receive affection. Being able to feel a wide range of emotions. Being spontaneous. Ability to put oneself in other people's shoes.

Other Strengths: Humor. Being able to laugh at oneself and take kidding. Liking to explore new horizons or try new ways. Willingness to take a risk with people and in situations. Perseverance. Having a strong desire to get things done and doing them. Ability to manage money. Knowledge of languages or different cultures through travel, study, or reading. Ability to make a public presentation. Making the best of one's appearance by means of good grooming and choice of clothes.

Step 2: Focus on the Specific Deed Rather Than the Doer.

Although we may not approve of a student's behavior, each always deserves our respect as a person. No better motivation can be given than clearly identifying a student's positive behavior. Avoid making statements such as, "you are terrific... wonderful... super... lovable." The problem with such comments is that students may assume that the converse is also true—that when they do not please us, they must be terrible, worthless, unlovable. As we clearly point out what students are doing that is positive, they will be encouraged and motivated. This concept is illustrated in Figure 5.5.

Step 3: Use the Language of Encouragement.

Teachers can maximize motivation by communicating clearly. Minimizing our own opinions and values and helping students grow to believe in themselves is the key to success in the encouragement process.

Action	Focus on Doer	Focused on Deed
A student turns in a neat paper.	"You're wonderful"	"I really like how clear your paper is. It will be easy for me to read."
A student volunteers for a difficult assignment.	"That's super."	"I like the way you accept challenges."
A student offers to help explain an assignment to	"You're so considerate."	"I like the way you think of others and offer to help them when you have work of your own."

Figure 5.5. Comparison of focus on doer and on deed. From *The Growing Teacher* by Carlson & Thorpe (1984), Prentice-Hall, Inc. Reproduced with permission.

Phrases that demonstrate belief in the student:

"I like the way you worked that problem through."
"I like the way you dealt with that."
"I'm pleased that you enjoy reading."
"I'm glad you're satisfied with the project."
"Since you are not satisfied with the project, what do you think
    you can do so that you will be pleased with it?"
"You look pleased."
"How do you feel about it?"

Phrases that display confidence:

"You'll work it out."
"I have confidence in your decision-making skills."
"You'll finish it."
"Wow, that's a tough one, but I'm sure you'll work it out."
"Knowing you, I'm sure you'll do fine."

Phrases that focus on helping and strengths:

"Thanks, that was a big help."
"It was thoughtful of you to _____ ."
"Thanks, I appreciate _____ ,
   because it makes my job easier."
"I really need your help on _____ ."
"You have skill in _____ .
   Would you share it with the rest of the class?"

Phrases that recognize effort and progress:

"I see you're moving along."
"Wow, look at the progress you've made!" (Be specific and tell
   how.)
"You're improving at _____ ." (Be specific.)
"You may not feel that you've reached your goal, but look how
   far you've come!"
"It looks as though you've really thought this through."
"It looks like you really worked hard on your homework."

In a classic presentation, Reimer (1967) lists ten specific
"words of encouragement" which further help to illustrate the
encouragement process.

1. *"You do a good job of...."*

Children should be encouraged when they do not expect it,
when they are not asking for it. One can point out some
useful act or contribution in each child. Even a brief
comment may have great importance to a child.

2. *"You have improved in...."*

Growth and improvement is something we should expect from all children. They may not be where we would like them to be, but if even a little progress has been made then the chance for discouragement is less. Children try if they can see some improvement.

3. *"We like (enjoy) you, but we don't like what you do."*

Often a child feels disliked after a mistake or misbehavior. It is important to distinguish between the child and the behavior, between the act and the actor. This is also known as "separating the deed from the doer."

4. *"You can help me (us, the others, etc.) by...."*

To feel useful and helpful is important to everyone. Children want to be helpful; we have only to give them the opportunity.

5. *"Let's try it together."*

Children who think they have to do things perfectly are often afraid to attempt something new for fear of making a mistake or failing.

6. *"So you do make a mistake; now what can you learn from your mistake?"*

The focus is upon a learning experience and future effort.

7. *"You would like us to think you can't do it, but we think you can."*

This applies when the child says that something is too difficult. Our expectations should be consistent with the child's ability and maturity.

8. *"Keep trying. Don't give up."*

When a child is trying, but not meeting much success, a comment like this might be helpful.

9. *"I'm sure you can straighten this out* (solve this problem, etc.), *but if you need any help, you know where you can find me."*

Adults can express confidence that children are able and will resolve their own conflicts when given the chance.

10. *"I can understand how you feel* (not sympathy, but empathy), *but I'm sure you'll be able to handle it."*

Sympathizing with another person seldom helps; rather, it suggests that life has been unfair to that person. Understanding the situation and believing in the child's ability to adjust to it is of much greater help.

The success or failure of these encouraging remarks will be a direct function of the teacher's attitudes and purposes for using them.

Many teachers find that creating a study group around the topic of encouragement is helpful. Through *The Encouragement Book* (Dinkmeyer & Losoncy, 1980), teachers have been able to develop their own sense of encouragement, as well as encouragement skills.

SUMMARY

The consultant has procedures that can help teachers change beliefs and develop different approaches to working with students. In addition to individual consultation, we believe working with teachers in both educational (STET) and problem-solving (C groups) groups is effective. Teachers can learn the skills of effective teaching and how to incorporate them into the daily teaching process. Every teacher-student relationship benefits from a clear understanding and utilization of encouragement. The consultant stresses a positive encouraging approach.

REVIEW QUESTIONS

1. Describe how teachers blame parents for problems with students.

2. How can consultants eliminate the "useless triangle?"

3. Discuss how groups can affect a lack of experience.

4. Identify the "C's" of a C group and how this process operates.

5. How can a consultant use encouragement in individual teacher consultation? In group teacher consultation?

6. List examples of effective and ineffective teacher beliefs.

7. Describe how consultants can help teachers change their faulty beliefs.

8. In what skills do teachers need to be proficient? How does STET teach them?

9. What is the special language of encouragement? Can teachers really use these words?

10. In what ways do praise and encouragement differ?

REFERENCES

Albert, L. (1989). *Cooperative discipline: How to manage your classroom and promote self-esteem.* Circle Pines, MN: American Guidance Service.

Baruth, L., & Eckstein, D. (1982). *The ABCs of classroom discipline.* Dubuque, IA: Kendall Hunt Publishing.

Carlson, J., & Jarman, M. (1975, Summer). Parent counsulting: Developing power bases and helping people. *Psychology in the Schools.*

Carlson, J., & Thorpe, C. (1984). *The growing teacher: How to become the teacher you've always wanted to be.* Englewood Cliffs, NJ: Prentice-Hall.

Dinkmeyer, D., Jr. (1980). *Teacher perceptions of discipline problems.* Unpublished research.

Dinkmeyer, D., & Dreikurs, R. (1963). *Encouraging children to learn: The encouragement process.* Englewood Cliffs, NJ: Prentice-Hall.

Dinkmeyer, D., & Losoncy, L. (1980). *The encouragement book.* New York: Spectrum.

Dinkmeyer, D., McKay, G., & Dinkmeyer, D., Jr. (1980). *Systematic training for effective teaching.* Circle Pines, MN: American Guidance Service.

Glenn, S., & Nelsen, J. (1987). *Raising children for success.* Fair Oaks, CA: Sunrise Press.

Lewis, J., & Lewis, M. (1989). *Community counseling.* Pacific Grove, CA: Brooks/Cole Publishing.

Painter, G., & Corsini, R.J. (1990). *Effective discipline in the home and school.* Muncie, IN: Accelerated Development.

Reimer, C. (1967). Some words of encouragement. In V. Soltz (Ed.), *Study group leader's manual.* Chicago: Alfred Adler Institute.

Chapter **6**

DEVELOPMENTAL CLASSROOM CONSULTATION

In this chapter, you will learn:

- a definition for developmental guidance,

- a rationale for "primary prevention,"

- a comprehensive developmental guidance program,

- procedures for training teachers, and

- how to identify effective resource materials.

Are we fitting round pegs into square holes, or should we change the holes? Students may need diagnosis, therapy, individual or group counseling, and special classes. The decisions to test, counsel, or refer are part of the school's environment. Often consultants help children to adjust to this structure within the school. Consultants also may successfully resolve student problems by modifying the social setting of the school. The school's structure can be changed. Consultants are concerned with the total school environment, examining ways to change not only the individual but also the system.

Chapter 6   Developmental Classroom Consultation   171

Developmental guidance, the focus of this chapter, co-exists with diagnosis, counseling, and therapy. It cooperates with these functions, or preferably helps to reduce their need in the school system. Perhaps our approach to developmental guidance can be characterized by a question and series of answers.

Why do children go to school? To delight in learning! However *naïve* or simple such an answer may seem, it clearly identifies the purpose of our educational system. It is a realistic goal for our children.

The consultant encourages students to learn and to help them in effectively applying their learning to life. The total learning environment is assessed. What promotes or interferes with the learner's abilities? To reach this goal, the consultant works with the significant adults in the child's life — teachers, parents, and administrators. Consultants cannot ignore adults. The teacher and parent influence every child six to eight hours each day. Consultants may have access to only six or eight students each day without the developmental approach.

A mathematical illustration is appropriate. An elementary school teacher with twenty-two students in a five hour day has 110 "influence hours"; per week, 550 "influence hours"; per year, at least 18,150 "influence hours" with the class. If the teacher refers a single student to a consultant who works with that student for ten one-half-hour sessions, five hours of influence occur; equivalent to one teacher day. This is 1/165th of the teacher's access to the single student and .000275% of the teacher's influence on the entire class.

The approach we advocate, "developmental" or "primary prevention," is a position shared by others:

> One is hesitant to suggest that any monolithic approach to guidance and counseling is the answer. Yet the time has come for us to emerge as a profession whose major tenets are growth—not problems—whose

practice arise from a study of what are normal biological and psycho-social growth patterns. Counseling has little to gain and perhaps even less to contribute if it continues to insist on using the clinical psychology approach and its problem-centered emphasis. (Muro & Miller, 1983, p.258)

PRIMARY PREVENTION

The term "primary prevention" identifies the approach to working in the schools as described in preceding paragraphs. In this chapter, a comprehensive primary prevention approach for the classroom is presented. Developmental activities are part of a primary prevention program.

For a mental health professional or consultant to wait in an office for problems to walk in the door is ineffective. Primary prevention is a comprehensive strategy that influences the "normal" and "not normal" school population.

Primary prevention

- Reduces developmental problems;
- is based in Adlerian or another developmental psychology, not just one or two isolated goals; and
- requires the cooperation and involvement of the significant adults (teachers, parents, and administrators) in the child's life. (Dinkmeyer, Jr., & Dinkmeyer, 1984)

A brief view of the medical profession offers a parallel. Some of the greatest medical breakthroughs of this century have been the development of preventive vaccines. In our lifetime, polio, smallpox, and other crippling childhood diseases have been eliminated or greatly reduced. The medical profession did not wait and treat each polio victim. Instead, elimination or control of the cause of polio was a more effective strategy.

The counseling profession has a parallel belief. Gerler (1976) reviewed more than 200 articles on counselor training and job experience. One-third of the articles favored an increase in primary prevention services. Not a single article advocated a decrease. Training in these services becomes part of the consultant's education. However, Schmidt and Osborne (1981) found that primary prevention procedures are not part of most counselor education training experiences. Advocacy for primary prevention is apparently not supported by actual training experiences. Conyne (1987) wrote a book entitled *Primary Preventive Counseling: Empowering People and Systems.*

Ten years after Gerler's review, the profession continued to advocate a preventive and developmental role for the counselor. A review of ten volumes (ten years) of the journal *Elementary School Guidance and Counseling* by Wilson (1986) documents this attitude.

The editorial leadership of the major journal in elementary school guidance, *Elementary School Guidance & Counseling* (ESG&C), also has endorsed a developmental approach. Don Dinkmeyer, who served as editor of ESG&C for the first 6 1/2 years, is a chief proponent of the developmental guidance movement (e.g., Dinkmeyer, 1966, 1971; Dinkmeyer & Caldwell, 1970; Muro & Dinkmeyer, 1977). More recently, Robert D. Myrick contrasted the efficacy of developmental and crisis counseling in his editorial, "Forms of Loneliness," which appeared in the May 1976 issue.

Yet, crisis counseling can be discouraging work. It is a band-aid that eventually becomes soaked with tears of unproductive loneliness and pulls away ineffectively.

A more productive approach is that of developmental guidance and counseling, a philosophy that ESG&C has embraced over the years. Developmental guidance helps people at all age levels learn before crises how to become aware of themselves and others, how to draw more on their personal skills and resources, and how to cope with situations in a responsible way. (Wilson, 1986, p. 212)

Developmental guidance skills often parallel elementary school counselor skills. These skills apply to any consultant at the elementary, junior, or senior high school level.

Although developmental guidance has been advocated for twenty years, the approach is not without its critics. This criticism includes the position that guidance counselors should not function in a developmental capacity. The political and social climate of the schools may not favor this approach; however, a paucity of research documents developmental guidance effectiveness.

The literature does not measure the extent of developmental counseling in the schools, but it does measure attitudes and interests. Wilson's (1986) review of October, 1973 through April, 1984 showed 117 developmental (35.2%), 129 remedial (38.9%), and 86 unclassified (25.9%) articles.

> Only about one-tenth (11.1%) of these articles, [advocating developmental guidance] however, provided evidence of the efficacy of a developmental procedure or activity in terms of statistically significant findings. Moreover, there is some indication that the number of developmentally oriented articles that include such documented evidence may be declining. (Wilson, 1986, p. 213)

The literature on developmental counseling gives a perspective. For the consultant, this history is interesting, and almost discouraging. We believe primary prevention and development of positive mental health can be delivered by a counselor or any of the other mental health professionals serving as consultants at the classroom level. The classroom, site of these primary prevention and developmental experiences, must be examined.

WHAT IS A CLASSROOM?

When children walk into the classroom, creative potential can be lost if conformity is expected. Academic achievement in standardized test scores, while an admirable goal, cannot be the only goal of quality education. In the classroom, consultants have the greatest resources and can make major contributions.

Learning can be improved by enhancing the psychological setting. Value can be enhanced by focusing on the climate in the classroom. The consultant can become involved with the learning climate. As we enter the classroom, we will see twenty or more students.

How can the consultant help the teacher reach every student? A useful procedure is to recognize that they are a group. By using group dynamics, an understanding of the interactions among children and between children and adults, the consultant can help students to learn to cooperate with each other. They can learn to value the unique contributions of each individual to the development of the group.

Teachers also benefit from a group approach. They can begin to see similarities between themselves and other teachers. The consultant helps teachers to strengthen students' self-esteem, social, emotional, and academic needs. This can be accomplished in an atmosphere characterized by

1. a mutual respect and trust by teacher and child;

2. a focus on mutual goal alignment by teacher and student;

3. students feeling that they belong to the group;

4. an environment that provides safety for the child;

5. an emphasis on self-evaluation in addition to evaluation by others;

6. a climate marked by identification, recognition, acceptance, and appreciation of individual differences; and

7. an emphasis on growth from dependence to independence.

The preceding list is representative, not comprehensive. It allows the consultant to identify methods to create effective classroom learning atmospheres. The list reflects psychological principles of individuals in groups (the student's movement in each group setting). A goal of developmental guidance is the understanding of self and others. These goals are succinctly summarized by Dinkmeyer and Dinkmeyer, Jr.:

Developing an understanding of self and others is central to the education process. The ability to understand oneself and others is a vital, yet often neglected, part of the elementary-school curriculum.

Children are at once thinking, acting, and feeling beings. Their thoughts and actions always involve feelings. They may like some subjects, be excited about and interested in certain media, dislike doing routine drills, be angry with a certain teacher, or be intensively involved with a project.

The feelings that accompany learning have a significant effect on how well children learn. If they have positive feelings, children tend to participate with a high degree of motivation and involvement and are more likely to derive permanent gains from their efforts. If children's feelings are negative, they are poorly motivated, participate minimally, and are less likely to derive permanent gains.

The classroom has great potential either to build or to erode self-concepts. Thus, if education is to accomplish its goals, systematic attention must be paid to the affective as well as to the cognitive domain. Self-understanding and social awareness are a vital part of effective, basic education (Miller, 1977). Elementary education, by virtue of its objectives, must plan for the development of the whole child.

The elementary-school years significantly influence the educational development of children. Studies have suggested that few factors are more relevant to the children's academic success and social development than their feelings of personal adequacy and self-acceptance (Combs & Soper, 1963; Coopersmith, 1959; Davidson & Lang, 1960; Fink, 1962; & Walsh, 1956). More specifically, Wattenberg and Clifford (1964) state that "In general, the measures of self-concept and the ratings of ego strength made at the beginning of kindergarten proved to be somewhat more predictive of reading achievement two years later than was the measure of mental ability."

Since the affective and cognitive areas of learning are interdependent within the person, they always operate simultaneously, even when the stated emphasis in the curriculum is on only one or the other objective. For example, the ability to listen to others can be radically affected by an individual's vocabulary and language skills

Education can no longer proceed on the assumption that when content is presented through interesting methods, the student will become involved, and the problems of delinquency, rebellion and apathy will be reduced dramatically. Instructors who do not get in touch with the whole being of students will not be able to meet the challenges of education and are destined to fail. (Dinkmeyer & Dinkmeyer, 1982, pp. 12-13)

We have characterized the current situation and the faulty assumptions about children and learning that limit the development of human potential. We also have presented a theory of learning and human behavior. However, a philosophy and a theory of learning and human behavior will be of little value if one fails to systematically organize classroom education. A number of authors have spotted the critical lack of humaneness in the educational process. However, despite their theorizing and pleading, little change has occurred.

A central problem in reorganizing schools is recognizing how dehumanized the educational system has become. We can document this dehumanization in many areas. The communication between administrative and supervisor levels and teaching staff is often reduced to formal memos, reports, projects, or objectives.

The tendency to minimize informal contact between administration and staff is illustrated by adversarial contacts between school boards and staff. Board members often think of the staff in terms of statistics, positions, and salaries.

A reduced emphasis on developmental education can be traced to several factors. Some schools, by departmentalizing at an early stage, bring the child into contact with large numbers of teachers, reducing contact with a single adult. Our premise is that education must be based on a belief in the dignity of all persons. If we develop a system that is dehumanized from the top to the bottom, neither the teacher, the parent, nor the child will have a model that encourages them to function on a more personalized basis.

If we value grades, authoritarianism, and content, we want a system different from values of responsibility, independence, involvement, and an open and positive attitude toward learning. One of the goals of this approach is to provide each child with a teacher who is concerned and interested in facilitating the human potential of every child. As a result of this concern, the teacher seeks to both understand and treat the child as an individual.

The teacher organizes the classroom group to facilitate the development of both the individual and the total group. Anything less than this type of commitment on the part of the teacher results in a dehumanized system. Humaneness has little chance of being developed in a system that is basically dehumanized.

FACTORS THAT BLOCK HUMANNESS

Three basic factors impede humane development: lack of goal alignment, inappropriate evaluation, and lack of context.

Mutually determined and **aligned goals** are desirable. The goals in many school handbooks are often different from teacher plans. Paper objectives bear little resemblance to actual classroom activity. Teacher's goals must be taken into consideration in the planning for educational experiences of children. Each teacher should be treated with mutual respect. As a professional, the teacher studies curriculum, the child, and methods for administering, organizing, testing, and evaluating educational experiences.

This approach is different from the current tendency to make changes in response to educational innovation and fads. The procedure for **appropriate evaluation** of students and the school's success can be an obstacle. It often focuses on cognitive development and functions as if education objectives can be assessed solely through achievement tests. If a student is reading, spelling, and doing arithmetic at a given level, this is one measure of success. But is the student truly an effectively functioning human being? A meaningful measure of educational philosophy, objectives, and teaching methods does not stop at the cognitive sphere.

Education is more than the accumulation of information. This learning occurs within a **context** that includes

- the student;
- the student's peers;
- the teacher; and
- their beliefs about self, and others.

Ignoring the feelings, context of learning leads to many of the negative classroom experiences we have outlined. This can be illustrated in the common experience of failure in mathematics.

If this (and other subjects) is taught in an atmosphere where mistakes are emphasized, where everyone is literally "on the same page," students dislike the subject. If I am not doing well in arithmetic, what does this imply about myself as a person? What am I feeling about myself?

Our feeling about what we can learn directly influences whether we cognitively grasp the ideas. Everyone has experienced academic failures that influenced affective feelings about their abilities in that subject. For some students, the unpleasant feelings pervade most subjects, and the schooling experience "teaches" one to be a failure.

Failure to appreciate and *use* the context of learning blocks most consultation efforts. Another aspect of the context of learning is understanding the group.

UNDERSTANDING THE GROUP

Each child is a member of the class or group. The social meaning and context of their behavior are important. If the teacher believes student behavior can be controlled by seating charts, verbal directives, and other techniques, the group context in which each child exists is ignored.

Four Principles of Group Interaction

Four principles of group interaction are to be considered:

Students Are Social Beings. Each child wants to belong to clubs, form friendships, and be a peer group member. Few want to be left out of groups, unless they are extremely discouraged. Students are members of at least three groups: family, class, and friends. This social interaction is inherent in human behavior, regardless of titles placed on any group. Everyone needs to belong to groups.

All Behavior Has Social Meaning and Purpose. Each student's behavior reflects a search for a unique place in the group. Finding this unique place can be challenging.

The social meaning and purpose (the goal) of the behavior, or misbehavior, does not have to make sense to the consultant. For example, Kate is a child who repeatedly talks to her neighbors, yet always stops when her teacher reminds her to be quiet. What could be the purpose of this behavior? Is she trying to get everyone's attention?

By using the simple technique of misbehavior goal identification, her teacher can "make sense" of this misbehavior. The goals each student adopts express the beliefs about how they belong in a classroom group. The private logic behind goals does not have to make sense to the teacher, and the student does not have to be aware of the goal.

Life-style Is Expressed through Behavior. The student's behavior is the means through which the goals of life are presented. If a student is not doing well in one area of work but seems capable of the work, what goal is the student pursuing? If we look to external reasons, we may find some legitimate factors. Nutrition, distractions in family life, or personal conflict may be a contributing factor. A more helpful procedure is to look at the internal reasons; the individually chosen behaviors which express the life-style.

Often the student is expressing a *choice*. For example, it may be a choice to do well, or do nothing at all, in any area of life, regardless of ability. Faced with challenges in a particular subject, the student may give up. From the student's point of view, it makes sense. It is consistent with the context of beliefs about self. A simple rule applies to all persons: ***Look at what a person does, not what they say***. This can be characterized as "Trust only movement."

Consider the following examples of actions and words:

- A teacher expresses interest in your suggestions, says she will use them in the classroom, but reports the next week that she wasn't able to find time.
- A friend says, "Let's have lunch soon," but never calls.
- An administrator agrees you need more time for planning, but continues to give assignments which make planning impossible.

In each example, words and actions are inconsistent. Behaviors are a more useful and accurate indication of the person's intention. Trust only movement.

Stimulating Social Interest Is Essential. Social interest is a willingness to cooperate for the common good of the group. If Becky wants to do a classroom chore such as feeding the pet or cleaning the chalkboard, she is expressing social interest. When a student is not willing to cooperate in the classroom (fighting, defiance, sullen withdrawal, or other disruptive movement), a teacher's response frequently is referral to the counselor, or expulsion from the classroom for varying lengths of time. Such actions only reinforce the student's faulty belief about a place in the group.

Students want to belong to the group at any cost, even if that place is in the principal's office. Later in this chapter, ideas for group cooperation and stimulating the social interest of discouraged students are presented.

Group Dynamics

Group dynamics is concerned with the nature of groups, their development, and relationships among individuals, groups, and institutions. Group dynamics is concerned with all forces affecting social change. Consultants operate with awareness of group dynamics. This cannot be incidental; it must be central to the consultant's role and function in the school.

The consultant is aware that the individual and the group are inextricably intertwined. The mixture of group and individual personalities should result in the development of a group of persons who are aware of these relationships and move toward a goal that is mutually acceptable. Understanding how to change a group can come from various perspectives. One perspective includes ten critical points for achieving change in the school.

Cohesiveness. Those who are to be changed and those who attempt to influence change must have a strong feeling of belonging to the same group. Through equal participation, a feeling of psychological interdependence must be developed.

Attractiveness. The more attractive the group is to members, the greater the potential influence of the group. This suggests that a critical issue is the selection of any group in the educational setting and doing things which enhance the attractiveness of the group. This is most often achieved by assuring that people who are socially powerful or attractive become members of the group. Attractiveness is also influenced by time and location of meetings and the strong support of administration.

For most consultants and teachers, selection of the group or classroom may not be easily achieved. In this case, the question becomes "What can I do to increase the attractiveness of this group?"

Values and Attitudes. In order to achieve change, one must identify which values and attitudes are the basis for attraction to the group. Those which are held in common can be used as forces for change. The group will have less influence on attitudes which are not related to the basis for group membership.

Prestige of a Group Member. The greater the prestige of a group member in the eyes of others, the more significant the influence. The implications for the consultant include the assessment of "prestige" of each group member.

Group Norms. Efforts to change individuals or groups to make them deviate from group norms will encounter resistance. The pressure to conform to group norms must be considered in any strategy to achieve change.

Perception of Need for Change. Everyone in the group should share perception of the need for change if the source of pressure for change is to lie within the group. Members must have a clear conception of purpose and personal commitment to individual and group goals.

Communication. Changing the group requires the opening of communication channels. All persons affected by the change must be informed about the need for change, plans for change, and the consequences of change.

Change and Strain. Changes in one part of a group produce strain in other related parts. This strain can be removed only by eliminating the change or readjusting the parts. Frequently a change in the substructure, such as a pairing of friends or opponents, will create increased tension in the total group.

Goals. Some of the most significant forces in the group include goals, aspirations, leadership, anticipations, attitudes, and cohesiveness. In order for a group to become meaningful, a group goal must emerge. Unless the group is working toward some announced goal, it will tend to be unproductive until the goal is clarified.

Aspiration. Moderate but realistic increases in the level of aspiration tend to generate a comparable increase in performance. Aspirations are essential to a group that wants to succeed, and they tend to result in both individual satisfaction and increased group performance. Therefore, moderately increasing the level of a group goal will usually result in a corresponding increase in the level of group performance.

THERAPEUTIC FORCES IN GROUPS

To discuss therapeutic forces in developmental classrooms may seem strange. These forces help us understand the need for a climate of growth, cooperation, and understanding. They are "therapeutic" in the sense they contribute to the well-being of the classroom. Time spent developing these attributes contribute to the overall benefit of the group.

In Figure 6.1 are presented nine forces important in the development of a healthy group. The following discussion presents the important aspects of each therapeutic force.

Acceptance

The skill of acceptance and mutual respect is the cornerstone of an effective, helpful classroom. If the teacher or consultant can share the ideas of reflective listening, this is promoting acceptance. We don't think this is appropriate for the younger grades, but at some point (usually much earlier than we initially think), students are capable of listening and responding to others' statements.

If students are too young for this activity, the ability to expand the feeling word vocabulary can be a step in this direction. Students can work on expressing themselves with more than the same old "mad, glad, sad, or bad" feeling words.

Mutual respect can be stimulated by the following specific activities:

- Students can pick a classmate to know better, through a talk about interests, siblings, or hobbies. Then each student introduces the partner to the rest of the class. If students are too young to introduce each other, the teacher can spend time each week introducing one of the students, focusing on these same areas of interest. Most students enjoy being the center of attention and through this activity develop an appreciation for the similarities and differences between classmates.
- Discussions where each student shares one personal strength, and finds one strength in a classmate.
- Encouraging empathy among students by simply noticing when they are being sensitive to each other. In addition, modeling of empathy by adults sets the stage for these behavior and attitudes in the students.

Ventilation

Students express emotions in the classroom, whether we "permit" this to occur or not. In a democratic or effective classroom, students feel free to share their feelings, which can be promoted by

- expanding the feeling word vocabulary,
- sharing appropriate feelings through I-messages,
- noting opportunities for students to share unexpressed emotions, and
- holding discussions which have as a focus the sharing of feelings.

During a classroom day, week, or month, many different emotions are experienced. The purpose of acceptance and ventilation is to give these emotions an opportunity to be expressed.

(Continued on page 190)

Force	Purpose	Example
Acceptance	To develop mutual respect and empathy among group members.	"I can see you're being sensitive to Joshua's feelings."
Ventilation	To acknowledge and promote the expression of feelings, often by using reflective listening.	"You seem very angry about this idea."
Spectator learning	To help students understand their own concerns as they listen to other group members discuss similar concerns.	"How can you apply our discussion of Jim's problem to your brothers and sisters?"
Feedback	To let students know how others perceive their behavior, often by encouraging the use of I-messages.	"Could you please tell Carlos how you feel when he teases you?"
Universalization	To help students become aware that they are not alone in their concerns, that most students have similar concerns.	"Who else has wondered about that?"

Reality testing	To let students experiment with new behavior.	"Let's role-play this problem and try out new ways of dealing with it."
Altruism	To encourage students to help each other, rather than compete.	"Beth, I really appreciate your helping Ricky with the math problems."
Interaction	To foster students' social skills and help establish an encouraging classroom atmosphere.	"Meg, please share with Joyce how you felt when she said she enjoyed playing with you at recess."
Encouragement	To simulate students' courage and social interest. To help students become more optimistic about solving problems.	"I think your study habits will help with your project."

Figure 6.1. Therapeutic forces in groups. From *Systematic Training for Effective Teaching* (STET): *Teacher's Handbook* by Dinkmeyer, McKay, and Dinkmeyer, 1980, American Guidance Service, Inc., Circle Pines MN 55014-1796. Reproduced with permission.

Spectator Learning

Students can learn from each other's similar concerns. The value is in discussing problem situations, because doing so allows that problem to be discussed simultaneously, allows other students with similar concerns to "learn as a spectator." Topics for such learning experiences include, but are not limited to, test anxiety, disappointments about jobs, concerns for the future, handling rejection, learning how to make new friends, and how to solve problems.

Feedback

The purpose of feedback is to give students clues as to how they are coming across in the group. Self-awareness can be increased when feedback is used appropriately. Feedback does not blame, accuse, or expect change by the other party. It simply states how the person is being experienced by another person.

For example, a student is constantly interrupting in a small class discussion. Feedback from either the teacher or students would state, *"I feel upset when you dominate the discussion, because (I) others can't say what they want."* Although change is not expressed in this statement, the foundation for change is laid in the dissatisfaction.

Feedback is a term with which mental health professionals are familiar. It may even be overused or misunderstood. In our context, we see feedback as simply an expression of feeling without criticism but with the encouragement for change.

Universalization

A good group, or classroom, depends on how well students realize their similarities with each other. Universalization is the process of working with students so they can see these similarities. This can be expressed as follows:

- *"Has anyone else ever _____(referring to a situation likely to be experienced by others)?"*
- *"Who else has_____?"*
- Discussions of topics which are likely to have broad appeal for students. This is similar to the idea of spectator learning, and topics can be used to promote universalization.

Reality Testing

The opportunity to experiment with new ways to respond to people is reality testing. Although the concept sounds abstract, each of us "tests reality" anytime we do something different.

One of the best ways to make this part of a group is to have the group leader model the ability to try new things. In the lower grades, it may be through encouraging small steps and seemingly minor movements. In the upper grades, modeling the "courage to be imperfect" can be a good way to encourage reality testing.

Altruism

The process of encouraging cooperation at the expense of competition is altruism. Although competition is a necessary part of schools, it is overemphasized and has negative effects. Altruism is also known as *finding ways to help each other.* Fostering altruism is a process of creating opportunities for the students to help each other. A process as simple as a "buddy system" is, in a real sense, fostering altruism.

Interaction

Some teachers report they want the interaction to be polite and cooperative at all times. Encouraging positive interactions among students, such as opportunities to work together without supervision, fosters the opportunity for appropriate interaction.

Encouragement

Although we have left this group force as the last one, it is perhaps the most important. Focusing on strengths and assets, stimulating social interest, and increasing an optimistic attitude are all part of the encouragement process.

The nine therapeutic forces in groups can be forces for recognizing and encouraging positive behaviors in the classroom. The peer pressures of the classroom can be understood and used with the proper understanding of these group forces.

The usefulness of these forces is summarized as follows:

- The group develops its cohesiveness around guidelines for freedom and responsibility.
- Group members help set goals, make decisions, and institute changes.
- Whenever possible, students proceed at their own level, reducing competition and stressing cooperation.
- Students talk openly and honestly with each other, and the teacher and other adults in the school system.
- An atmosphere of mutual respect and trust is developed.
- Encouragement is the prime motivator.
  (Dinkmeyer, McKay, & Dinkmeyer, 1980, p. 187)

COHESIVENESS

Cohesiveness plays a significant role in group dynamics. The properties of a cohesive group include change both in the formation and maintenance of the group.

STYLES OF CLASSROOM LEADERSHIP

A useful procedure is for consultants to conceptualize the group leadership role as having three typical expressions: democratic (desirable), autocratic, or permissive (less desirable, but prevalent). Figure 6.2 presents characteristics for each of these three approaches to the classroom.

Note the style of leadership directly affects the atmosphere, or climate, of the classroom. Consultants can use this idea to help consultees assess their role in their classroom. For example, the consultee/teacher who is interested in benefits of feedback but has a permissive atmosphere may find that students misunderstand the idea and use it for "killer" communication, putdowns, or other inappropriate statements.

LEADING THE CLASSROOM: GROUP SKILLS

Classroom management techniques often focus on discipline strategies. They may be nothing more than containment procedures which attempt to stop disturbances, or keep them at an acceptable level. If teachers do not understand the purpose of behavior or have group skills, such techniques will not be successful. It reminds us of the acceptable but ineffective method of popping popcorn—leaving the lid off and standing nearby with a shopping bag!

(Continued on page 196)

Democratic	Autocratic	Permissive
Mutual trust. Mutual respect.	Control through reward and punishment. Attempt to demand respect.	Students may do what they want without concern for others.
Choices offered wherever feasible.	Demands. Dominates.	Anarchy.
Motivation through encouragement. Identification of the positive.	Focus on weaknesses and mistakes.	All behavior tolerated.
Freedom within limits. Balance between freedom to work and responsiblity to work.	Limits without freedom. Promotion of dependency and/or rebellion.	Freedom without limits. Confusion.
Intrinsic motivation. Teachers and students set goals together	Extrinsic motives and punishment.	Motivation erratic, unpredictable.

Success-oriented activities designed to build self-confidence.	Activities focus primarily on producing superior products.	Some activities help students make progress and others do not.
Cooperation, shared responsibility.	Competition.	Individual rights without regard for rights of others.
Discipline as educational process. Self-discipline encouraged.	Discipline is to establish external control.	No discipline is expected.
Goals are aligned.	Goals are set by teacher.	No positive goals.
Ask for ideas, contributions.	Teacher decides all issues.	No formal decisions reached.

Figure 6.2. Styles of leadership and classroom atmosphere. From *Systematic Training for Effective Teaching [STET]: Teacher's Handbook* by Dinkmeyer, McKay, and Dinkmeyer, 1980, American Guidance Service, Inc., Circle Pines MN 55014-1796. Reproduced with permission.

The beliefs and skills of teachers in classroom settings can be illustrated by the following example taken from Dreikurs, Grunwald, and Pepper (1971, p. 104). It is a classic demonstration of how many teachers mistakenly use "group discussions" to lecture and talk at pupils.

> Teacher: *I'd like to talk to you about our basketball. I repeat, "a basketball," not "a football." I am sure all of you know the difference. A basketball is meant to be thrown into a basket. That's why it is called a "basketball." This afternoon I saw some of you kicking it. Do you know what may happen when you kick it? It may get a hole in it and then we'd have to have it repaired. Do you know how much it costs to have such a ball repaired? It's not cheap, and the school will not pay for it. You know who will have to pay for it? You will. I know that you enjoy that basketball and wouldn't want anything to happen to it, so let's all be very careful how we use it. All right?* (Children nod their heads.) *I knew you'd see it my way, and I'm very proud of you."*

This teacher is trying to convey friendliness and confidence in the children. However, the teacher still resorts to "preaching." Chances are that the children pay little attention. The teacher might have said:

Teacher: *I must talk with you about our basketball. I know that you enjoy playing with it, but before we can take it out again, we'll have to make some decisions.*

Whose ball is it?

Children: *Ours.*

Teacher: *I am afraid it is not.*

Children: *It belongs to the school.*

Teacher: *That's right. We may use it, but we are responsible if anything were to happen to it. How can we prevent this?* (The children will now discuss various possibilities of how to use the ball so that no damage should occur.)

Teacher: *What should we do if any of the children should kick it?*

Children will then suggest a number of consequences that will make sense to the possible offenders. They may suggest that these children not be permitted to play basketball for a week or two. They may suggest that these children should pay for any damage they have done. The important thing is that students need to be involved in the discussion and decision making process.

LEADERSHIP SKILLS

Consultants must be able to use and teach specific group leadership skills. In the preceding example concerning the basketball, the skill might be characterized as "demanding." The result would have been predictable but ineffective.

An alternative to many common group leadership techniques is a specific set of group leadership skills which foster growth, independence, and responsibility. Teachers can learn these skills in educational groups, practice them in their classroom, and report to and receive support from the group members.

In Figure 6.3 are presented group leadership skills. The skills are equally appropriate for consultants when dealing with teacher groups.

Structuring

Structuring is the most important group skill. The leader establishes the guidelines for the discussion or activity, clarifies any misunderstanding, and states the purpose of the meeting.

(Continued on page 200)

Skill	Purpose	Example
Structuring	To establish purpose and limits for discussion.	"What's happening in the group now?" "How is this helping us reach our goal?"
Universalizing	To help students realize that their concerns are shared.	"Who else has felt that way?"
Linking	To make verbal connections between what specific students say and feel.	"Bill is very very angry when his brother is late. This seems similar to what Joan and Sam feel about their sisters."
Redirecting	To promote involvement of all students in the discussion and to allow teachers to step out of the role of authority figure.	"What do others think about that?" "What do you think about Pete's idea?"
Goal disclosure	To help students become more aware of the purposes of their misbehavior.	"Is it possible you want us to notice you?" "Could it be you want to show us we can't make you?"

Skill	Purpose	Example
Blocking	To intervene in destructive communication.	"Will you explain your feelings?" "I wonder how Stanley felt when you said that."
Summarizing	To clarify what has been said and to determine what students have learned.	"What did you learn from this discussion?" "What have we decided to do about this situation?"
Task setting and obtaining commitments	To develop a specific commitment for action from students.	"What will you do about this problem?" "What will you do this week?"
Promoting feedback	To help students understand how others perceive them.	"I get angry when you talk so long that the rest of us don't get a turn. What do others think?" "I really like the way you help us get our game started."
Promoting direct interaction	To get students to speak directly to each other when appropriate.	"Would you tell Joan how you feel about what she said?"
Promoting encouragment	To invite students directly and by example to increase each other's self-esteem and self-confidence.	"Thank you for helping us out." "What does Carol do that you like?" "Who has noticed Jamie's improvement?"

Figure 6.3. Group leadership skills. From Systematic Training for Effective Teaching (STET): Teacher's Handbook by Dinkmeyer, McKay, and Dinkmeyer, 1980, American Guidance Service, Inc., Circle Pines MN 55014-1796. Reproduced with permission.

Classroom Example: *"Let's talk about the damage to the bookshelves—we need to do something. Who'd like to start?"*

Teacher Group Example: *"The purpose of this group is to introduce new ideas you might use in your teaching, to practice these ideas, and to receive support from fellow teachers."*

Comment. Structuring is often understood as the art of stating the obvious. This is correct! Too often a discussion does not achieve its objectives when those objectives are left unstated. It's the rare meeting, discussion, or class activity which does not benefit from structuring statements.

Universalizing

Universalizing is the process of helping students realize that their concerns are shared. It can be verbalized by the comment *"Who else has felt that way?"* when the group leader senses that the topic has been felt or experienced by others. In teacher groups, universalization is a process, not a single comment. It is fostered by the consultant creating opportunities for teachers to share similar concerns and challenges.

Linking

Linking occurs when the consultant points out who has what in common. For example, the statement *"It seems like A and B have X in common"* is an effort to link A and B on the concept of X. Similar concerns which are often found as "X" concepts in teacher groups can be focused on the ineffective teacher beliefs discussed in an earlier chapter. For example, teachers are often concerned about getting students to cooperate all of the time, to be perfect, or to not make mistakes.

Redirecting

Redirecting occurs when the consultant wants the teachers to talk directly with each other instead of through the consultant as switchboard operator. If a teacher is directing a comment to another teacher, it should be directed to that teacher.

Goal Disclosure

Goal disclosure occurs when the group is working on behavior anecdotes. For each incident, the purpose is to guess the goal of the misbehavior.

Brainstorming

Brainstorming is the process of accepting all ideas when a solution is sought, without evaluating or negating any of the ideas. This can be particularly helpful when considering new strategies.

Blocking

Blocking is the important process of intervening in destructive communication. Consultants do not have to be solely responsible for blocking, but must set the tone through structure, rules, or modeling.

Summarizing

Summarizing can occur at any time, but is particularly helpful when one wants to learn what has happened in the group. This skill provides each member an opportunity to share what has been important. It also allows the leader to learn what has been important for the members. It can be started by the direction to complete the sentence, *"I learned . . . "*. Summarizing is an excellent opportunity for everyone to give an equal amount of time to the group.

Task Setting and Obtaining Commitments

Task setting and obtaining commitments relates to the process of making discussions and ideas into concrete, behavioral actions. For example, a student might say, *"I want to do better in that subject."* This is vague, and gives only a general intent. Task setting is the process of deciding what it will take to achieve the "better" in that subject. You also can help the entire class set tasks.

In teacher groups, we have found that teachers (consultees) have a similar tendency to have good intentions but not necessarily the ability to make their intentions specific. In this case, the consultant's task is to make the teacher aware of what will be different, as specifically as possible. General ideas such as *"I want to do better"* or *"My class should be more cooperative with each other"* have more specific counterparts, accomplished through task setting and obtaining commitments.

Commitments should be as behavioral as possible, and should be for a specific period of time. Be wary of statements such as *"I'll never do that again,"* or *"I'll try that idea."* Most consultation relationships have opportunities for follow-up; make the commitment for only the period of time between meetings. From this basis, the consultant and consultee can build some momentum toward their goals.

Promoting Feedback

Promoting feedback is the process of exploring how one is perceived by others in the group. It is directly related to the therapeutic force of feedback within groups.

Promoting Direct Interaction

Promoting direct interaction allows students to speak directly with each other. Instead of mediating in disputes, allow students to work out their differences.

Promoting Encouragement

Promoting encouragement is the process of finding what is right or okay in the teachers, and letting them know it. It is the ability of the consultant to find out the assets and abilities for each consultee. From that knowledge, encouragement helps the person to consider alternatives.

The process of memorizing these group forces and group leadership skills will not make one a better group leader or teacher. The process of working with groups with an awareness of these forces and skills does make one a better leader.

SUMMARY

Many consultation challenges involve teachers. A helpful procedure is to recognize a set of common and detrimental teacher beliefs concerning their part in the change process. A consultant then must decide how to deal with teachers, whether as a group or on an individual basis. If the group is used, several group forces can be used and group leadership skills will help to make it a productive problem solving and educational experience.

REVIEW QUESTIONS

1. What is guidance, and how does the consultant use guidance activities?

2. What does the term "primary prevention" mean? What does it imply for the consultant?

3. What are two principles of groups?

4. What are two therapeutic forces of a group?

5. What are two leadership skills?

6. Why would a consultant choose to use a group for delivery of consultation services?

REFERENCES

Conyne, R.K. (1987). *Primary preventive counseling: Empowering people and systems.* Muncie, IN: Accelerated Development, Publishers.

Dinkmeyer, D., Jr., & Dinkmeyer, D. (1984). School counselors as consultants in primary prevention programs. *Personnel and Guidance Journal, 62,* 464-66.

Dinkmeyer, D., & Dinkmeyer, D., Jr. (1982). *Developing understanding of self and others: DUSO 1.* Circle Pines, MN: American Guidance Service.

Dinkmeyer, D., McKay, G., & Dinkmeyer, D., Jr. (1980). *Systematic training for effective teaching.* Circle Pines, MN: American Guidance Service.

Dreikurs, R., Grunwald, B., & Pepper, F. (1971). *Maintaining sanity in the classroom.* New York: Harper and Row.

Gerler, E.R. (1976). New directions for school counseling. *The School Counselor, 23,* 247-251.

Muro, J., & Miller, J. (1983). Needed: A new look at developmental guidance and counseling. *Elementary School Guidance and Counseling, 17,* 252-260.

Schmidt, J.J., & Osborne, W.L. (1981). Counseling and consulting: Separate processes or the same? *Personnel and Guidance Journal, 55,* 339-354.

Wilson, N.S. (1986). Developmental versus remedial guidance: An examination of articles in Elementary School Guidance and Counseling, Volumes 8-18. *Elementary School Guidance and Counseling, 20,* 208-214.

Chapter 7

PARENT AND FAMILY CONSULTATION

In this chapter, you will learn:

- a rationale for working with parents,
- parent group education strategies,
- a problem-solving "C" group for parents, and
- an approach to family counseling and therapy.

INTRODUCTION

Parents and siblings exert the most significant influence on the development of the individual. The family is the arena in which love, trust, acceptance, and a sense of belonging are cultivated. Divorcing the family from the school setting, or the consultant's responsibilities, is unrealistic.

In this chapter, you will learn how to work with parents, whether in educational or therapeutic interventions. We stress the importance of preventive, educational programs and indicate how the consultant can establish these programs.

RATIONALE

With few exceptions, the family and, in particular, the parents exert the most significant influence on the development of an individual. The family is the arena in which love, trust, acceptance, and actualization are cultivated. The child's position in the family constellation and the relationship with siblings also exert a tremendous impact. If this structure is unhealthy, a negative and harmful influence results, characterized by fear and atypical growth.

Although the past three decades have seen, in our opinion, a lessening of many positive influences of the family, to ignore the tremendous impact of the family influences on personality development would be foolish. The influences of the family, both positive and negative, continue to have a profound impact on each individual in our society.

One has only to look back on our own personality to see the connections. For example, within the family environment is where the original meanings about life are obtained—the meanings of trust, love, adequacy, and acceptance. From this place within the family, a child perceives beliefs, customs, and myths and acquires many parental values. The family supplies the context for dealing with feelings of superiority and inferiority. In the family is where the individual formulates a view of self as a social, working, sexual, and spiritual being and develops fundamental allegiances with people.

The family becomes the first socializing agency as parents and siblings help the individual to develop an identity and to find a place in the world. The basic education of the individual in emotional and social areas first takes place within the family. *The family should never be underrated in terms of its effect upon the learnings of the individual.*

PARENT EDUCATION

Parents rarely have adequate experience, training, and educational background to enable them to function effectively in their role as child caregiver. Many parents, who are largely unequipped for the role, play the most significant role in the development of society.

An employment ad in the classified section of your newspaper might read, "WANTED: guaranteed employment for 15 to 20 years. Invest $80,000 to $125,000 of your own money, long hours, immense challenges, satisfaction not guaranteed. No prior experience or education required..."

The imaginary advertisement accurately depicts the nature of the parent job responsibilities. When you work with parents, you work with employees who have been "hired" for this job. Our efforts as consultants to parents can focus on the educational opportunities.

In the Adlerian approach to parent education, normal or adequate parents are given an opportunity to increase their skills with their children. One need not necessarily be sick, deviant, or troubled to be assisted by a consultant.

The attitudes, ideas, and interrelationships of parents are frequent sources of problems. The struggle involved with obtaining independence from their own autocratic background or permissive patterns does not help parents to establish democratic approaches to deal effectively with their children. The acquisition of new techniques in democratic management of children is no longer a matter of choice, but of necessity. A healthy family unit is the most important ingredient in a healthy society.

Parent education is an increasingly important consultation function for school mental health consultants. It provides an opportunity, in educational settings, for maximum growth in the family. The attention given to the development of parent education programs has been increasing. Available programs in the parent education field give evidence of the growth of this particular dimension of the consultation field.

Schools have long emphasized the importance of working with parents and families of the students, but parent education is much different from some traditional vehicles for parent involvement. Organizations such as parent-teacher associations have been created to function in this area. Some significant issues, however, are not being met in this structure. When communication is established in other than this perfunctory manner, it is usually done in a negative or crisis situation such as behavioral problems or truancy. The need exists to involve parents in a positive program of mental health. Parents tend to involve themselves only when the purpose for involvement is clear and relevant to them.

Parental involvement must be beyond the typical one-time meeting, such as report card time or evening open house meeting. What is needed is a planned program of parent education. Any program of consulting, counseling, or remediation that proposes to help an unproductive person must contain mechanisms for bringing about changes in family relationships. Traditionally, the school has not provided assistance in helping families to establish policies and principles related to human behavior.

The consultant accepts the challenge of restructuring the school by seeing opportunities in the home and community. This role is perhaps best characterized as "an architect of change." Concern is with the whole child and therefore recognizes the importance of working with parents. Previous strategies have noted the resistance of parents to bring their real problems to school. The consultant deals with this by going to the parents, not only to listen to their problems, but to teach parents skills in solving problems.

Working in the actual life space of parents helps the family members to develop solutions to their problems. The consultant must go beyond just knowledge, as knowledge defines a problem and does not solve it. The consultant is eager and willing to help formulate ideas, but is not a judge, umpire, or dispenser of criticism.

A program of parent education which centers on weekly parent group discussions is also an integral component in allowing parents to take an active role. These groups are formed to help parents to understand and work with the affective and cognitive aspects of dealing with their children. Once a program of this nature is begun, it becomes self-supporting. Despite common misconceptions, our experience has been that parents (regardless of socioeconomic status, intellectual level, or ethnic background) want and will seek out and support this activity. Perhaps the effectiveness of parent education can be attributed to the many advantages that the participants derive:

- Parents find their concerns are often common to concerns raised by other parents.

- Consultants who do not have children do not have to answer the "How can you understand if you don't have kids?" questions, because within each group are many who are "qualified" in that aspect.

- Groups are opportunities for parents to learn from each other.

- Parent education is a method for new ideas, skill practice, and encouragement to place the new ideas and skills into each family.

- The parent education group is cost-effective, reaching not only the 10 to 12 participants, but their children and spouses. The sphere of influence while running the group is large.

Every consultant should be well acquainted with the parent education materials that are currently available and be a competent parent education leader. Consultants who are interested in reaching the greatest number of persons will develop a training program which permits them to train additional parent education leaders. Most of the current parent education programs are well organized and come with detailed leader's manuals.

Two programs which focus on parent education through book study illustrate the concepts discussed in parent education groups.

Children: The Challenge

Children: The Challenge (1964), by the eminent Adlerian psychiatrist Rudolf Dreikurs and his colleague Vickie Soltz, was perhaps the first significant material used in the parent education field. The book presents Dreikurs' thinking on parent-child relationships.

It deals with the dilemma in the autocratic/democratic society and then outlines a method of understanding and encouraging children, identifying their mistaken goals, how to develop and maintain relationships with teens, how to win cooperation and avoid giving undue attention to misbehavior. The numerous, brief chapters are often used in discussion groups.

Raising a Responsible Child

Raising a Responsible Child (Dinkmeyer & McKay, 1973) was a significant book for individual and group study, more contemporary in nature. The book deals with the Adlerian approach to understanding human behavior, promoting emotional growth. It gives greater attention to the mistaken concepts of adults and children which interfere with effective parent-child relationships. The book expands the Adlerian approach to include information on communication skills, how to listen more effectively, and explore alternatives.

Considerable attention is also given to encouragement and logical consequences. Sections deal with games that children play and also approaches to problems that children have at school. This book has a guide for effective problem solving when parents are seeking solutions to particular situations.

Although book study groups continue to help many parents, there are inherent limitations to this approach. Book study groups require a high level of skill training by the consultant or group leader. Simply because a book is well-written is no assurance of a good group experience.

In addition, these books are written without illustrations, cartoons, clarifying charts, or other aids which would make them more visually interesting to the parent. These two factors make book study groups available to a smaller portion of the parent population than can be reached through formalized parent education programs.

Systematic Training for Effective Parenting (STEP)

The STEP (Dinkmeyer & McKay, 1989) program is the most widely used Adlerian parent education program. STEP and its companion STEP/Teen for the parents of teenagers have reached approximately three million parents, either in parent education groups or through their own reading.

The STEP program is organized so that consultants can teach the program the first time and then start to identify parents who with a minimum of training can become facilitators of the program. Consulting becomes most effective as the leaders are permitted to have a leadership role and an opportunity to train additional numbers of parents.

The content of the STEP program focuses on nine major concepts:

1. Understanding children's behavior and misbehavior.

2. Understanding more about your child and about yourself as a parent.

3. Encouragement: Building your child's confidence and feelings of worth.

4. Communication: How to listen to your child.

5. Communication: Exploring alternatives and expressing your ideas and feelings to children.

6. Natural and logical consequences: A method of discipline that develops responsibility.

7. Applying natural and logical consequences to other concerns.

8. The family meeting.

9. Developing confidence and using your potential.

The STEP program is organized systematically as a skill-building program. The program has a systematic instructional sequence. The process usually involves a discussion of a previous week activity assignment. Parents are asked to do something specific with their children or in observing their children and then report back on the results.

A discussion is held of the assigned reading, focusing mostly on how this reading applies to working with their children. The charts are visual aids which set forth the major concepts and principals of the program and the chart is discussed to reinforce the major concepts.

Parent education groups often consist of approximately one dozen members, meet once each week for about one-and-a half to two hours, and meet for six to nine weeks. Attendance is usually voluntary, although we find increasing use of parent education as part of the judicial system's attempts to remediate abusive and neglectful parents. Most groups are closed; when a group begins, no new members are allowed to join a group in progress.

While the mix is heterogeneous, the recommendation is that parents have at least one child of about the same age so that themes of common challenges particular to an age group can be enhanced. For example, the parents of a teen are often bored by discussions of bed-wetting or the challenges of toddlers. Similarly, parents of toddlers are often horrified to learn of the challenges of adolescence to greet them in a decade!

Systematic Training for Effective Parenting of Teens (STEP/Teen) has the same philosophy and psychology as the STEP program. The content adds material to help the parents understand personality development and emotions in adolescence as well as understand their own emotional responses. The STEP/Teen program also goes into much greater detail with the special challenges that occur during the teen years (Dinkmeyer & McKay, 1989).

A third program, *Early Childhood STEP*, has been developed for parents of younger children, ages birth to six (Dinkmeyer, McKay, & Dinkmeyer, 1989). A companion for STEP and STEP/Teen, the program offers similar concepts at age-appropriate levels. For example, the age range is divided into three areas: babies, toddlers, and preschoolers. Specific developmental information is presented so that parents know what to expect from their children.

THE LEARNING CYCLE
IN PARENT EDUCATION GROUPS

Parent education groups function successfully when the consultant understands areas of leadership skill, the learning cycle, and the stages of the group.

Leadership Skills

1. Structure the group's time, topics, size, and scope. Most parent groups meet for one to two hours. Usually 10 to 14 parents are in each group, and the group meets once each week for six to nine weeks (several chapters can be compressed, if necessary). The topics of the group should be structured to reflect the educational nature of the group. The group is not therapy.

2. Seek to universalize the experiences of the group members. Most parents have had similar challenges raising their children: bedtime, chores, motivation are examples of typical issues. However, parents usually do not recognize their experiences are similar to others in the group. The group leader has the task to point out how their experiences have been similar.

   Another avenue for universalizing is expectations for their children. Most parents want their children to do well in life, to learn from their mistakes, and to try hard. These goals can be explored, and methods for reaching them are a purpose of the parent education group.

3. Encourage, encourage, encourage. You can never be too encouraging with parents in the group. Even when court-ordered, discouraged parents are in the group, the leader must seek to find what is right or okay about these parents. Simply being in the group is an asset which can be acknowledged.

The Learning Cycle

1. New ideas are presented through discussion of the readings and charts. In most chapters, the ideas presented are new ones, compared to more commonly used ideas. For example, in the chapter on motivation the new idea of encouragement is contrasted with the idea of praise.

2. The ideas are then translated into specific skills. If the parents understand the idea of encouragement, how do they encourage? What is said or done that is encouraging? Parents practice the skill through role-play, problem situations, and audio or videotaped incidents.

3. The importance of using the skills with children is stressed through practical applications. In most group meetings, the consultant makes certain parents know what their homework for the week will be. This can then be checked and discussed at the start of the next group session.

Stages of the Group

1. "Great Expectations." The parents are usually excited and involved, but believe the group will teach them how to "fix" or change their children. Group leaders should spend time structuring the group so that parents understand the goals of the group. Universalizing is also necessary to allow members to begin to recognize the commonality of their concerns. This stage of the group often lasts two to three sessions.

2. "You mean I have to change?" Here parents begin to recognize that the parent group offers ideas to change themselves, not the children (although changes in children do result as a consequence of the parent's new behaviors and attitudes). Parents who have no interest in changing their behaviors may become discouraged. This transition stage is an opportunity for the consultant and leader to understand human behavior and encourage any positive movement.

3. "Cohesiveness and commitment." The final stage of the group is characterized by cohesiveness and a commitment to change. Many groups find it difficult to end, because the experience has been beneficial for the participants.

The Next STEP

The Next STEP (Dinkmeyer, McKay, Dinkmeyer, Dinkmeyer, & McKay, 1987) is an advanced program designed for parents who have completed *STEP, STEP/Teen,* or *Early Childhood STEP.* It provides a basic introduction to concepts while developing a problem-solving procedure. The program is organized to help parents apply the STEP concepts to specific problems. In the course of the program an opportunity is provided for parents to become more familiar with their own life-style and how it affects their parenting effectiveness.

Optional content is available to be covered by a particular group. Some of the options include building your and your child's self-esteem; your child as an achieving person; learning to make responsible choices; gentle strength and firm love; discipline; special concerns of parents of infants, primary, and toddlers; special concerns of intermediate teens and handicapped children. Units are also devoted to stress in the family and the issue of single parents and step-parents.

The Parent C Group

The "C" Group is a method for helping group members acquire knowledge and evaluate their own beliefs and attitudes. This concept was originally developed for use with teacher groups and explained in Chapter 5. In the "C" Group, there is an opportunity to go beyond the study of principles and involves the showing of not only procedures and ideas, but also helps members become more aware of how their beliefs, feelings, and attitudes affect their relationship with their children (Dinkmeyer & Dinkmeyer, 1976).

The power of the "C" group comes from the parent's awareness that a belief such as "I must always be right" or "No one's going to challenge my rules" interferes with effective relationships and caring communication. Parents are helped to see that their belief results in resistance and struggle for power. However, if the belief is modified to "I prefer to be right, but I can make mistakes" or "It would be easier if my authority wasn't challenged as part of growing up," then the possibility for conflict resolution is increased.

Leaders of "C" groups prefer to work with parents who have been in study groups or STEP groups since a common awareness of the fundamentals of human behavior and common ability to use basic parenting skills exist. In the "C" group the leader then integrates this awareness with their feelings, beliefs, and attitudes to apply the principles to very specific situations. Leaders of "C" groups require much more skill in utilizing group dynamics in dealing with problem solving.

The approach was titled "C" group because the forces that make it effective begin with a C. The specific components include:

1. Collaboration. Working together on mutual concerns as equals is a basic requirement.

2. Consultation is received and provided by the members.

3. Clarifying of member's beliefs and feelings is accomplished.

4. Confrontation produces more honest and realistic feedback. A norm is established so that each individual sees his or her own purposes, attitudes, and beliefs and develops a willingness to confront other members with their beliefs.

5. Concern and caring permeate the relationship.

6. The group is confidential. Whatever is discussed within the group stays within the group.

7. Commitment requires that each person make a decision to participate fully and become involved in working on his or her own personal concern.

8. Change is the purpose of involvement and each member determines his or her goals for change.

THERAPEUTIC FORCES IN PARENT GROUPS

The group provides a unique opportunity for all parents to become more aware of their relationship with their children. They are allowed to experience feedback from other parents in regard to the impact that their parent procedures have upon their children. This opportunity for mutual therapeutic effect is constantly available. Concurrently, provision is made for the creation of a strong bond which takes advantage of the universal problems that confront parents. They experience a realization that "all parents have problems" and that solutions are available. The opportunity for parents to help each other and to mutually develop new approaches to parent-child relationships is provided. Corrective feedback from peers has a tremendous effect upon the participants.

The consultant who conducts parent groups must be careful not to establish the group as if its intentions were to provide information and to deal only with cognitive ideas. This is not a lecture, nor is it a discussion, but truly a group experience. This necessitates the use of group mechanisms and dynamic processes that are present in any well-organized therapeutic group. A primarily educational group can have therapeutic results.

The consultant realizes the necessity of assuring and encouraging parents (even if only by their good intentions to help the child). The consultant should lead, not push or tell. The parent group is much different from the traditional parent meeting. The parent group emphasizes the treatment of parents as "whole people" and as equals. They are not lectured at or told how they should be, but are dealt with in relation to their own concerns and to where they are at.

Some of the group mechanisms which are particularly pertinent to group work include the following:

1. Group identification or a communal feeling. The idea that all are concerned about common challenges, and a willingness to help parents live more effectively with their children.

2. The opportunity to recognize the universal nature of child training problems.

3. Opportunities not only to receive help but to give assistance, help, and love to others. The opportunity to develop cooperation and mutual help, to give encouragement and support.

4. The opportunity to listen which not only provides support, but in many instances provides spectator therapy. Someone else's idea may enable parents to start a new approach to transactions with their child.

5. The mechanism of feedback—the individual gains from listening to and observing others.

ADLERIAN FAMILY COUNSELING

The Adlerian approach feels that most parents mean well but have faulty methods of child training. Therefore, the focus is on providing parents with specific principles and not generalities. Adlerian centers such as child guidance centers and family education associations provide parents with the opportunity to observe practical demonstrations. Parents get involved in group discussions on how to apply these principles to a specific family.

All in attendance are provided an opportunity to learn more effective ways of relating with their children. This is accomplished through observation and identification with the family receiving counseling. Many of the normal problems parents have with children are universal and center around meals, sleep, and dressing. Therefore, in this approach, parents are able to understand their own situation when they observe it in another family. Because of their lack of emotional involvement with children in another family, they can be more objective and understanding of what is occurring.

While the Adlerian approach is based on the assumption that parents and children need to develop new family relationships, the emphasis is to provide education and training—not treatment. The focus is on teaching parents more effective techniques and helping adults and children to become aware of purposes of their misbehavior.

Sessions for parents begin with an introductory meeting where rationale and procedures are explained, questions answered, and a voluntary commitment made. Usually evening meetings of one-and-a-half hours are scheduled. Once a rapport has been established, the interview with selected parents before the group is carefully structured.

The volunteer parents may be asked to describe the routine of a typical day, such as the misbehavior of a child and reactions or actions of the parent. The counselor continually includes other parents in the group in this discussion. Involvement of other parents is usually limited to guesses about what might be "true" about a child, based on their birth order position or shared behavior incident, and checking this out with the parents. The intent is to be helpful, to gain a better understanding of the family dynamics.

Then, the counseled parents are asked to leave the room, and the children are brought in to clarify hypotheses made about the children's goals. After the children talk, the playroom director may contribute observations about the children in play situations and the teacher may describe the children's classroom behavior. The parent group is then asked for action suggestions, and these are discussed and sorted according to significance.

The characteristic elements of the Adlerian approach in a public demonstration are as follows:

1. The focus of attention is directed toward the parents, as the parent is generally the problem, not the child. The child responds only in his or her own way to the experiences to which he or she is exposed. Especially younger children do not change easily as long as the parent's attitudes and approach to the child does not change.

2. All parents participate simultaneously in a procedure that may be called "group therapy." In these sessions each case is openly discussed in front of other parents. Many parents gain greater insight into their own situation by listening to the discussion of similar problems which other parents have. In this way an influence is exerted beyond the scope of individual treatment and the whole community, including teachers, is directed toward a better approach to understanding and handling children.

3. The same therapist works with parent and child. All problems of children are problems of a discouraged parent-child relationship. The therapist is confronted with this relationship and must approach it from both ends simultaneously. Working with one party alone is almost a handicap. The speed and course of treatment depend upon the receptivity of parent and child alike. It can be evaluated only if the therapist is in close contact with both.

4. The problems of the child are frankly discussed, regardless of his or her age. If the child understands the words, this child also can understand the psychological dynamics which they describe. Contrary to widespread belief, young

children show an amazing keenness in grasping and accepting psychological explanations. In general, much more time is needed for a parent to understand the psychological dynamics of the problem than the child; the child recognizes them almost immediately.

5. If other children are in the family, all of them are discussed, not only the "problem child." These problems are closely related to the behavior of every other member of the group. One has to understand the whole group and the existing interrelationships, the lines of alliance, competition, and antagonism to really understand the concept and behavior of any one member.

6. The main objective of our work is the change in the relationships between child and parent, and between or among siblings. Without such a change, altering the child's behavior, life-style, approaches to social living, and concepts of self in relation to others is impossible.

Although family counseling and family counseling demonstrations require a high level of skill, an interesting point to note is similarities in steps in the process. The group model provided a pattern for parent education, and the concepts are also used in family therapy. A consultant in a school setting would do well to consider the advantages of the family counseling demonstration center as a part of a complete set of services for the community.

FAMILY THERAPY

In this section the concepts for Adlerian family therapy are outlined. The term therapist and consultant are used interchangeably. While not all consultants would perceive themselves as therapists, understanding the principles behind effective family interventions is helpful. This section may serve as a frame of reference when evaluating referrals to other community professionals. In this section, we outline a strategy which seeks to change the family system in the most direct and economical techniques.

Understanding the Model

Adlerian family therapy is a specific intervention strategy. One benefit of this approach is the large number of concrete procedures for understanding the family. Patterns, goals, and movements within the family are all viewed as possible routes for understanding and improving the family. The consultant, counselor, or therapist is seen as leader in the relationship. This means he or she would formulate questions and give suggestions which first identify and then reframe the family system.

The concrete procedures and techniques which help to change the family system include extensive use of consultation and parent education. The goal of this model is to change the system (or group) which the family has created, and to help each individual function within that new system.

History and Development

The tradition of family counseling is strong within Adlerian psychology. Adler established clinics for the purpose of couple and family counseling. He began these in Vienna in 1922; eventually more than thirty were created. One of the most interesting aspects of these centers was the emphasis upon public demonstration. Adler's work is the predecessor to the public family counseling described in the preceding section of this chapter.

Adler and others would counsel or advise a family in a public forum, not in private. This was in stark contrast to other approaches to working with families. In the counseling demonstrations, the therapist might work with members of the family as subsets; for example, beginning with the parents, then all of the children at once, followed by the parents, and then the entire family. If this was therapy, the family might be seen as a whole for the entire session.

The purpose of the Adlerian approach was threefold: to help the family, to demonstrate to other professionals how to work with families, and to help others understand that their concerns were similar to those being raised by the demonstration family. These demonstrations were the precursor to the family education centers now found across North America, and modern Adlerian family therapy.

Adler continued his work with public demonstrations for several years. His efforts were cut short by the chaotic events which preceded World War II. Adler and others were forced to leave Europe and continue their work in other areas, such as North America and Scotland.

The influence of Adler's work cannot be minimized. A widely used textbook puts Individual Psychology in this perspective:

> Alfred Adler was far ahead of his time, and most of the contemporary therapies have incorporated at least some of this ideas... The Adlerian viewpoint is applicable to a wide range of human relations, including but not limited to individual and group counseling, marital and family therapy, and the alleviation of social problems. (Corey, 1986, p.65)

Corey continued by listing contributions of Adlerian theory to the existential, person-centered, Transactional Analysis, behavioral, Rational-Emotive, and reality therapies.

Rudolf Dreikurs, a student of Adler, came to Chicago in 1937. He established a Child Guidance Center at Abraham Lincoln Center and other centers across the Chicago area. Dreikurs trained counselors in many other parts of the world, encouraging the creation of Family Education Centers (FEC). Centers were created in more than 20 cities throughout the United States, Canada, and in many other countries.

Many of these FECs continue to operate, and new FECs have been established since Dreikurs' death. In many communities, the FEC is a referral source for Adlerian family therapy. Dreikurs had a profound commitment to making Adlerian Psychology available to the public. While in Chicago, he founded the North American Society of Adlerian Psychology (NASAP) and the Alfred Adler Institute of Chicago (now Adler School of Professional Psychology), institutions which continue to serve Individual Psychology throughout North America (Dinkmeyer & Dinkmeyer, 1991).

Dreikurs made a significant impact on the way in which the authors of this book work with families, whether in therapeutic or educational settings. His work on the four goals of misbehavior is a simple yet elegant example of his profound insight into the nature of children's behavior. When complimented about this concept as a "brilliant invention," he is reputed to have replied, "I did not invent them, I simply saw them!". Such was the power and influence of Dreikurs' work.

Major Theoretical Concepts

A useful procedure is to see each family member with the following characteristics:

- indivisible
- social
- creative
- decision making
- goal-directed beliefs and behaviors

This view is holistic. It looks for patterns, unity, and consistency.

All Behavior Has Social Meaning. The social context of behavior has been discussed in prior chapters, but it also applies to the family and the relationships within that system. A child's poor school work makes sense when another sibling's excellence in school discourages this child. Father's refusal to do any housework affects not only mother, but all children who see non-cooperation as an acceptable male value.

Another concept essential to understanding social context is socially useful behavior, or social interest. Examples of socially interested behavior in a family include cooperation, completing assigned or volunteered tasks, and looking out for the welfare of others. While many immediately understand this as the responsibility of the adults in the family, it is also the opportunity for the children and teens of the family to move toward responsible behaviors.

The concept of social interest has profound opportunities for the therapist or consultant. If the family is not cooperating or is dysfunctional, an area for homework or education may be one in which social interest is stressed. Thus, social interest will also be a barometer of the relative health or progress of the therapeutic or educational intervention. In short, if they are getting better, are they doing things for each other?

All Behavior Has a Purpose. As previously stated, all behavior has a goal. The movement toward a goal is revealed in a person's behaviors.

Goal-directed behavior in the family is explained by Sherman and Dinkmeyer:

> The family therapist can become aware of goals by examining her feelings or by having the members involved in the transactions examine their actions and reactions. For example, in a parent-child conflict, the parents feels annoyed and the parent devotes much time to the child. It may be the child is attempting to seek the parent's

attention. However, if the parent feels challenged and would like to prove that the child cannot do that, it is likely that a power struggle will ensue. And if the parent feels hurt, the child's desire to get even will be apparent. Feeling utter frustration or the need to rescue, the parent will know that although the child is capable, he is displaying inadequacy in order to cause the parent to give in and do for him. (Sherman & Dinkmeyer, 1987)

Striving for Significance. We seek to belong in a significant way, in a way which moves us from a perceived minus to a perceived plus. For all children, especially in the first years, we are "less than" by virtue of our age and corollary physical, intellectual, and emotional abilities. The efforts of young children to belong in the family can be assisted if parents and therapist can find ways for these children to contribute, significantly, in positive ways. The opposite of this would be the youngest child who constantly gets his or her way by whining or demanding. He or she is a "significant" disruption in the family, and his or her striving for belonging is seen as a mistaken assumption.

Subjective Perceptions. The point of view of each family member is a fertile ground for the therapist:

> It is essential that the therapist understand the perception of the family members. Each person develops and is responsible for his or her subjective view of life. People give all of their experiences meaning. This process has been described as follows: Each person writes the script, produces, directs, and acts out the roles. We are creative beings deciding our perceptions, not merely reacting. We actually often elicit responses which help us to maintain our self-perceptions, including negative ones. (Sherman & Dinkmeyer, 1987)

Adlerian Family Therapy System

Adlerian family therapy is an interactional, or systemic, treatment model. It is not an individual approach that has been adapted to family therapy. What happens between family members is crucial to the Adlerian therapist. The basic principles focus on the social meaning of behavior, purposive behavior, and the movement between and among individuals.

Understanding the family means working with the family as a group. Family interactions are guided by the goals, life-styles, and private logic of each member as well as the group goal, life-style, private logic, and family atmosphere.

Dinkmeyer and Dinkmeyer (1991) suggested the family interacts around eight dynamic qualities:

- power and decision making
- boundaries and intimacy
- coalitions
- roles
- rules
- similarities
- complements and differences myths
- patterns and styles of communication

GOALS OF THE THERAPEUTIC PROCESS

The role of the therapist is not often perceived as one which fits a school consultant. However, recent events in our culture have made it more important that school personnel understand the basic methods of successful interaction with the family system.

To that end, we present a series of questions which may help the school consultant shape a role in the intervention or referral for the family. The questions were first introduced in Dinkmeyer and Dinkmeyer (1991) and have been modified to portray probable issues in a school setting.

1. What does each person want to have happen in the family? Can any of this be achieved by school personnel?

2. What does each family member see as the main challenge or issue faced by the family?

3. Are family members aware that the purpose of these sessions is to focus on change, not merely to complain?

4. Do they understand the nature and duration of the contact with the school consultant?

5. Identify where the family stands on developing family cohesiveness, cooperation, community, and satisfaction. This can be accomplished through questions such as the following:

   a. What is the level of self-esteem? Does each family member have a sense of worth? Does each feel valuable, capable, loved, and accepted?

   b. What is the level of social interest? Does each family member have a sense of belonging, a feeling that they are part of the group? What is the commitment to cooperation, involvement, and sharing?

   c. What is the sense of humor that exists in the family? Can family members see themselves in perspective? Can they make jokes about themselves, accept their mistakes, have the courage to be imperfect, avoid nagging supervision and defensiveness?

6. What roles do various members play in the family? Are they functioning in a variety of tasks, or does each family member have certain restricted roles to play in the family?

7. Who is for or resistant to change? It is important to understand who is seeking change. Are they willing to change themselves? What is the type of change they want in the family, in individuals, and in themselves? Equally important is to analyze and identify who it is that is

resisting change. Clarify the purpose of the resistance and what the person gets for that resistance.

8. The traditional approach is to become involved in the diagnosis of family faults, weaknesses, and psychopathology. Even more important is the diagnosis of the assets of the family. What are the general assets of the family as a unit? What are the assets of each family member? How do they blend into the family system? What resources are available in the extended family and community?

Family Change

Change in the family can include:

- The uses of power can be redirected.
- New understanding and insight.
- New or refined goals.
- New skill knowledge or options, particularly in communication, problem solving, and conflict resolution
- Increased courage and optimism, a sense of empowerment.
- Increased social interest.
- New roles within the family system.
- Commitment to growth and change.

(Sherman & Dinkmeyer, 1987)

Most of the changes can occur in successful therapy, or successful counseling, or successful education. A basic principle of the Adlerian approach is to involve the family at the least expensive, least intrusive level appropriate to their needs. This requires a clinical or professional judgment on the part of the school personnel.

SUMMARY

In this chapter, we have presented a comprehensive approach to working with parents. This approach includes parent education, family counseling, and family therapy. The consultant serves as a resource for creating parent education programs. If qualified, the consultant also can conduct family counseling. The consultant needs to understand concepts of family therapy. Within these concepts lies an understanding of the role of Adlerian psychology for all family members.

REVIEW QUESTIONS

1. What is the rationale for consultation with parents and families?

2. Name two approaches to working with parents.

3. What is the "3 step" cycle of parent education, and what does it imply for the consultant's intervention?

4. What are therapeutic forces in parent groups?

5. How can a "C" group be used with parents?

REFERENCES

Corey, G. (1986). *Theory and practice of counseling and psychotherapy* (3rd ed.). Monterey, CA: Brooks/Cole.

Dinkmeyer, D., & Dinkmeyer, D., Jr. (1976). Systematic parent education in the schools. *Focus on Guidance, 8*(10), 1-12.

Dinkmeyer, D., Jr., & Dinkmeyer, D. (1991). Adlerian family counseling and therapy. In A. Horne (Ed.), *Family counseling and therapy* (pp.383-401). Itasca, IL: Peacock.

Dinkmeyer, D., & McKay, G. (1973). *Raising a responsible child: Practical steps for effective family relationships.* New York: Simon and Schuster.

Dinkmeyer, D., & McKay, G. (1989). *Systematic training for effective parenting of teens.* Circle Pines, MN: American Guidance Service.

Dinkmeyer, D., McKay, G., & Dinkmeyer, J. (1989). *Early Childhood STEP.* Circle Pines, MN: American Guidance Service.

Dinkmeyer, D., McKay, G., Dinkmeyer, D., Jr., Dinkmeyer, J., & McKay, J. (1987). *The next step: Effective parenting through problem solving.* Circle Pines, MN: American Guidance Service.

Dreikurs, R., & Soltz, V. (1964). *Children: The challenge.* New York: Hawthorn.

Sherman, R., & Dinkmeyer, D. (1987). *Systems of family therapy: An Adlerian integration.* New York: Brunner/Mazel.

Chapter 8

CASES ILLUSTRATING CONSULTATION IN SCHOOLS

Authors' Note

The following seven cases illustrate consultation challenges. We have numbered the statements within each transcript to assist class discussion.

As you read these cases, keep in mind:

- What is the purpose of the consultation?
- What goals do the consultee and the student pursue?
- What do you think of the consultant's plan?
- What other plans are possible?
- What would you do, and why?

These cases provide readers with an opportunity to learn from the consultant and consultee. Equally important, each case allows the reader to learn from the discussion questions at the end of each case.

CASE 1
MRS. DAVIDSON AND THE JUNIOR HIGH
SCHOOL MATH CLASS

Authors' Introductory Comment

The following case describes how a consultant can help a junior high school teacher. The consultant appears to have gained very positive results despite an ineffective communication style.

Presenting Problem

Mrs. Davidson is a junior high school math teacher who is beginning her second year of teaching. She received a bachelor's degree from a small midwestern college many years ago and has recently gone back to teaching. Her daily schedule includes five class periods of eighth graders. She is a mild-mannered woman who has little discipline, control, or organization in her classroom. She is the brunt of many jokes, does not raise her voice, ignores most of the activity in her room, and tries to teach the few interested students.

Approach to Problem

The consultant began individual sessions with Mrs. Davidson:

C1: *A few of your students from second period spoke with me this morning and they seemed upset. Is it a particularly rough group to handle?*

T1: *They're no better or worse than the others. I'm so unhappy and I just don't know what to do.*

C2: *What do you see occurring in the room that upsets you?*

T2: *I know they make noises, faces, and they just don't care about math.*

Mrs. Davidson relates several incidents that suggest disruptive behavior because of classroom boredom and lack of interesting or stimulating classes.

T3: *They just don't like me, they'll try anything.*

C3: *Mrs. Davidson, do you like your students?*

T4: *How can I? If you had to put up with the circus I do every day—how can I like them?*

C4: *Then why tolerate it? Why do you think this atmosphere exists?*

T5: *I guess because we don't know or care about each other very well.*

C5: *What do you think you could try to change the environment in the room?*

T6: *I don't know. I'm not sure anything would work now, but I've thought about it before.*

C6: *Are you willing to try something new?*

T7: *I guess so, but I'm not really sure.*

C7: *Why don't we stop thinking about a new environment but take a long, hard look at what's going on now, and then try a few things.*

T8: *Okay, I'll try.*

C8: *What are some things you have discussed or would like to try in your classes that isn't routine work?*

T9: *Oh, I was going to try and just talk to them a little, but you don't know what it is like in there.*

C9: *How about if I find out so we could better work together? Would you mind if I observed the class one day?*

T10: *No, I guess it's all right. I'll probably be a little nervous, though.*

After the class, both teacher and consultant reviewed the events that took place, how the teacher felt about it, and the students' reaction as well. Teacher and consultant discussed the feelings observed in the class, teacher reactions to several questions (bringing out her distance and lack of rapport), general boredom prevalent in the class, lack of interesting activity, routine assignments, and the consequential reaction to boredom expressed in disinterest and disruptive behavior. The session was a painful one for the teacher. Although she felt some relief in having discussed the problem, she was visibly upset. The consultant supported her recognition and acceptance of the problem.

C10: *I think you can do a great deal to help the situation. You are a compassionate person but you must involve students more in your class. You know your subject material very well.*

T11: *When Mr. Blake (principal) called me to his office, he just told me "you must crack down on discipline," but no one ever tells you how.*

C11: *Well, how would you like to begin?*

T12: *I really don't have any ideas, that's part of the problem.*

C12: *What would happen if you spent one class period and talked to your students honestly. Let them know you understand their feelings, explain how you feel about the situation, and recommend they explore ways to help change the environment. It may hurt as they'll be honest, but we've already discussed the points they'll probably raise, right?*

T13: *Well, yes, but what about the lesson for that day?*

C13: *Forget the lesson. If the students aren't with you, then what purpose does "today's lesson" have anyway?*

T14: *I think you're right. I'll try it but what should I talk about?*

C14: *Try what is most meaningful for you...look at some of these alternatives:*

  a. *Discuss the situation—set up discipline boundaries and enforce your limits.*

  b. *See what the students would like to see changed, then actively involve them in the change. Have discussions, make lists.*

  c. *Get them involved in the class and accepting some responsibility.*

  d. *Explore variety in program, board work, projects, puzzles, etc.*

  e. *Discuss the sequence...you don't have to teach every minute of every period. Include some interesting activities to wake the students up.*

T15: *I think I'll try it next week. Can we talk about some of these things before next week?*

C15: *Fine. How about we get together after school tomorrow and let's both jot down some ideas for that meeting.*

The teacher and consultant discuss philosophy and details on the "new classroom," and various ways it can be implemented. Several shorter meetings follow. Teacher reads two recommended books designed to broaden the scope of her teaching and encourage thought beyond course content. Teacher and Consultant discuss discipline boundaries, and how to enforce limits. Consultant suggested that they talk with another teacher and see how she handles control and discipline problems. This session was very meaningful because a new relationship developed between the two teachers, and Mrs. Davidson received some helpful ideas.

Results and Conclusion

Mrs. Davidson held her first day of "new" classes. During the first class she appeared nervous, but students were receptive. She was prepared for their comments and questions. They talked in smaller groups, listed things they'd like to see changed, and the teacher did the same. They discussed the lists, and she became more confident as the day went on. She also felt freer in talking to students. Students didn't know how to react to Mrs. Davidson.

Additional suggestions were discussed such as adding further variety to the program: math bees, math derbies, skits, using remedial programs, and help sessions. After the first two weeks, the teacher and consultant met on a less frequent basis. It was good support for the teacher, and the consultant could watch her slowly take over and create a new teaching style.

The following year, a consultant began teacher groups within the school and Mrs. Davidson became an active participant and outgoing member of the group.

Frame of Reference

The consultant in the previous situation observed events in the classroom and helped the teacher analyze the data. Given the situation, the consultant can discuss developmental methods to aid in the change of the classroom environment. The consultant should be competent enough in curriculum, evaluation, method of operation, and discipline to offer ideas for their modification.

The teacher, on the other hand, recognized the problem and was ready for change. She accepted the challenge of submitting herself to a confrontation with the consultant and then sharing her feelings with students. A new course of action was developed to better serve the needs of students and to create a more positive, enjoyable learning environment in the classroom.

Authors' Comments and Discussion Questions

1. In this case, the consultant and teacher did not seem to communicate in the beginning, and yet all works out well in the end. How can this be explained?

2. The consultant seemed to have a "hidden agenda" or purpose for the interview before it begins. He seemed to have viewed the problem from his point of view and has set out to convince and persuade the teacher. Is this a good idea? Do the ends justify the means?

3. The consultant begins the session by seeming to understand and by attempting to find out the teacher's point of view. At C2 the consultant does not seem concerned with the teacher's feelings and misses the teacher's message. How could the consultant show that he understands how the teacher feels?

4. The consultant seems more concerned with getting the facts or gathering data than directly dealing with Mrs. Davidson's problem. Do you agree?

5. At C3 the consultant again misses the teacher's feelings of aloneness and inadequacy. What might have been a more appropriate response?

6. At C3 and C4 the consultant is meeting his needs. He seems to be teaching. In your opinion, is it hard to apply the listening skills to teachers?

7. At T7 and T8 what happens? Does the teacher feel as though she is being heard?

8. In the discussion before C10, why did the consultant deal with his recognition and acceptance of the problem rather than her feelings or tears?

9. What do you think about the consultant's response at C11? What is the consultant concerned about?

10. In reviewing the transactions T11, C11, T12, and C12, do you feel that consultant and teacher are communicating?

11. Do you think that the teacher could do what the consultant requested at C12?

12. The consultant at C14 recognized the teacher's willingness to change but lack of knowledge about what to do. He begins to help the teacher by clearly specifying possible approaches.

13. How can the consultant help the teacher to become less dependent on him?

CASE 2
MRS. CONWAY AND THE HIGH SCHOOL HOME ECONOMICS CLASS

Authors' Introductory Comment

Mrs. Conway is overrun by her high-school-age students. The consultant clarifies the problem and systematically helps the teacher to develop skills and techniques with which to turn the situation around.

Consultee

Mrs. Conway, a beginning teacher, holds a bachelor's of home economics degree from a large metropolitan university and a diploma from a teachers college in another large city.

Presenting Problem

A home economics class, made up of boys from grades 9 through 12, was a serious problem to this teacher in her first year. She felt that the class was taking neither the course nor her seriously.

Approach to Problem

The consultant began individual consulting sessions with Mrs. Conway:

C1: *You were saying the other day that you were having trouble with one of your classes.*

T1: *I have trouble with one art class and one home economics class.*

C2: *Let's look at one class and see what is happening.*

T2: *They can't get into a routine.*

C3: *This is the home economics class?*

T3: *They just treat it as a big joke and because it's not needed for their programs they could not care less about their marks. There is no way I can encourage them.*

C4: *You seem to feel you are battling with them and they are treating it as a joke and not taking you or your course seriously?*

T4: *Right. So I figure I must be doing something wrong. What am I going to do about it?*

Teacher describes some measures she has taken, none of which have helped, and gives a brief description of the class composition.

C5: *Generally, you have a core who want to work and others who are disrupting.*

T5: *Right, but I can't pick out the others. I should be able to, but this class has been so disruptive that I find it even hard to associate names and faces and seats in the seating plan. There are probably 10 or 12 I should boot out, but I can't pick them out specifically as trouble-makers. They all seem to be going at once.*

C6: *Well, now that we have the general picture, could you give me a specific example of what happened during class one time?*

T6: *I try to keep talking all the time about things we're doing and that are related to table-setting and buying. When I got to table-setting, that again initiated a discussion about eating cereal with dessert spoons instead of little spoons.*

C7: *Was this done seriously?*

T7: *It began seriously but some think it's a big laugh and use anything they can to get the class going.*

C8: *And also to get you going?*

T8: *I really try not to get upset.*

C9: *So when they started to talk again, what did you do?*

T 9: *That was the third time during the demonstration. I said "That's it!"*

C10: *What did you do?*

T10: *I left the demonstration table, took off my apron, threw it in the box, and pointed over my shoulder and said, "Clean it up."*

C11: *You were really annoyed?*

T11: *I was annoyed to the point that my voice cracked. It's the first time my voice has cracked.*

C12: *You've been annoyed before, but this time you were angry.*

T12: *Yes. I was mad. I don't have to put up with this. They have to learn there's a time to fool around and a time to work, and they also have to learn when they are pushing me too far and that I can be pushed too far. So they will be more careful.*

C13: *What did they do then?*

T13: *I sat at the desk and the boys started to clean up. Then I said to myself why should I stay here, if anyone comes I am so mad that I'll yell, or my voice will crack.*

While teacher describes similar incidents, consultant emphasizes action in class, teacher action, resulting action in class, and teacher's feelings as well as focusing on her talking and reminding.

C14: *About how many times have you said this in the last five-period cycle?*

T14: *I have said the same thing every lab since the beginning of the term. I don't think one has gone right.*

C15: *With all your reminding it hasn't improved? Has sending them to the office helped?*

T15: *No, it doesn't make a bit of difference.*

C16: *You're open to suggestions. There are two things I would like to suggest. First, you need to integrate your class. You have those who want to learn and those who don't want to learn. The problem is to motivate the latter. These sociometric group choice forms to rearranging the kitchen unit groups might help.*

Consultant describes how to use the sociometric forms and arranges to meet with teacher for assessing and making up groups.

C17: *Another suggestion is a class discussion. Now you are talking a lot and it isn't doing any good. Sit down with them and say that you can't continue with the class this way. Approach it from the point of view of what can we do about it and come to an agreement with the class.*

T16: *Tomorrow would be a perfect time to do both of these.*

C18: *Now how would you like to go about this? Would you like me to come in?*

T18: *I would just like some pointers.*

C19: *When you sit down you should be in a circle for a discussion so that everyone can see everyone else. Begin by saying that you can't make them do anything they don't want to do. In that way you are not in the position of trying to be boss. Say that you are sitting as equals. You have a job to do but can't do it the way things are going. The purpose of sitting together is to see what the problem is: what we can do about it and come to an agreement about some of the things we will do about it. Listen to the suggestions of the non-motivated ones just as much as to the others. Listen to all suggestions and find out what they can agree upon. You can always say that you are not going to remind them so much because they know what is expected.*

T19: *The thing I suspect is that they won't come up with any suggestions except why can't we cook meals.*

C20: *Well, you can say that we can't do anything about the cooking but we can do something about what is happening in our class.*

C21: *How do you feel about this now?*

T21: *That it's all right.*

Results and Conclusion

The next day the consultant met with the teacher to show her how to use the sociometric data she had obtained from the class to select new groups. She reported that she also had a class discussion in which points of conflict were discussed and some changes agreed upon.

After two weeks she reported a marked improvement in the class and within a month she described it as an "ideal class" assuming responsibility for doing demonstrations and disciplining themselves with the teacher serving as a guide. Having reduced the talking to a minimum, she no longer needs to remind them about routines.

The teacher who now has regular discussions with all her classes has shared this positive experience with other staff members.

Authors' Comments and Discussion Questions

1. At C4 and C7 the consultant concentrates on clarifying the problem.

2. At C9, C10, C11, C12, and C13 the consultant demonstrates some good consulting leads to get to specific anecdotes.

3. At C16 and C17, the consultant makes direct suggestions for the teacher to do. Is this an acceptable practice? Are there more effective ways to do this?

4. At C18 we see the consultant following through on the commitment of the teacher to find out if she really knows what to do. This procedure in a two to four week period in which the consultant actively monitors the new behavior of the teacher enhances success.

5. An interesting point to note is how the words "try" and "do" indicate one's level of commitment. "Try" is usually a partial commitment, while "do" is a more definite statement of one's intent to follow through. In this example, the teacher at T8 had been "trying" and in T16 she was going to "do."

6. This incident quite dramatically illustrates what occurs in classes in which the teacher still feels that she holds the authority. The consultation session between the consultant and the teacher is rather lengthy and appears to have dealt with a substantial amount of irrelevant information. The extent to which the consultant can quickly come to an understanding of the dynamics of the situation is important. This is a minor criticism of the consultant's approach. However, today with the high ratio of students to consultants, time becomes an important factor.

7. The consultant in a situation such as this should be able to quickly obtain an adequate picture of the dynamics of the behavior by following a definite structure: (1) an

account of the nature of the observable behavior, (2) a brief description of the action that the teacher has taken, and (3) the response of the youngsters to the action. Armed with those data the consultant is in a position to help the teacher explore possible solutions.

8. The consultant's offer, "Would you like me to come in?" is a legitimate consulting approach. However, this type of help should be offered in cases where the teacher's relationship with the children has deteriorated to the point that it is impossible for the teacher to conduct a profitable discussion. Here, such an approach was unwarranted. The relationship between the teacher and the pupils had not totally deteriorated.

9. The consultant developed a good relationship with the teacher which encouraged and rebuilt her confidence in her ability to handle the incident. In incidents like this the teacher often errs by setting out to correct the problem before establishing a solid foundation, namely, a good class relationship. Here, the consultant has done an admirable job in laying the groundwork for the development of a good relationship by helping the teacher discover the first step in solving the problem: a discussion with the youngsters—"What are we going to do about this situation?" The consultation would have been enhanced, we think, by helping the teacher understand how to employ the sociometric survey. The teacher should suggest this approach in a discussion with the youngsters. The use of a sociometric survey as a means to obtain a diagrammatical picture of the social structure of the classroom is excellent. However, to enhance its validity, an important step is to insure that the youngsters understand the purpose.

10. In this particular case, the use of sociometrics should have been suggested during the discussion with the youngsters. A teacher who proceeds to use an instrument without discussion, consultation, and acceptance by the group is a teacher still imbued with the need to assert personal authority.

11. The discussion then should center on what needs to be done to establish a good working relationship, with the youngsters offering suggestions as well as the teacher. This indicates to the students that the teacher is willing to operate as an equal in the solution of instructional difficulties as well as the establishment of a just class procedure. The consultant could have brought that to her attention.

12. Continuous consultation appears not to have been used in this incident. Follow-up procedures are an important phase of counseling. A teacher may follow a consultant's suggestions, as in this case, developing a good class relationship with democratic procedures and find that the results are exceedingly rewarding, only to have the relationship atrophy. Follow-up consultations are often necessary to encourage the teacher in the proper use of the democratic approach in the classroom.

CASE 3
MS. RHODES AND CHRISTY C

Authors' Introductory Comment

This case presents a puzzled teacher, difficult child, and "tuned-out" consultant.

Presenting Problem

Ms. Rhodes is a third grade teacher, beginning her first year of teaching.

Christy C. is an eight-year-old girl in third grade who has puzzled the teacher by unpredictable behavior; sometimes showing disinterest in school activities, ignoring teacher directions to the class, and, at other times, writing ingratiating notes to the teacher and bringing her little gifts.

Family Atmosphere

The mother appears to be the head of the family; she is quite outspoken, and is very protective of Christy. She sees little of the children except on weekends because of a job and night classes. The family constellation is as follows:

Christy: She is eight years old, attends a parochial, inner-city school which attracts students from outside the area, as well as nearby. Christy and her brother come to school by bus.

Jimmy: A seven-year-old who attends the same school and seems to be achieving well.

Approach to Problem

The teacher approached the consultant with a new situation the teacher didn't know how to handle. She was already a member of a teacher C group (consulting group) and was aware of the rationale for the four goals of misbehavior.

T 1: *Look at this.* (A letter written by the child telling the teacher how much she, Christy, dislikes Ms. Rhodes.)

C 1: *Could you tell me what happened before she wrote this?*

Ms. Rhodes describes how the child seemed to be retaliating because she was sitting apart from the other children; that she was ignoring directions and had done no work all morning. When she was given a written punishment she began it, but wrote the note also.

C 2: *How did you feel when you read this? That could give us an idea of what Christy is up to.*

T 2: *I was really hurt.*

C 3: *This was different from just wanting attention, then. She seems to have a reason for wanting to hurt you.*

T 3: *What can I do?*

C 4: *We've talked about the goals of misbehavior, and you remember that something you should not do is allow yourself to show hurt.*

T 4: *I'm sure I did that already, but I can see it won't help.*

Discussion showed that a real struggle for power was apparent, the child showing that she would have her way. The possibility that revenge was a goal also was discussed.

T 5: *But what should I do this afternoon? I've already told her she has to do the work.*

C 5: *Could you ask her if she would rather work alone? If she has a choice, you would not leave yourself in a struggle for power.*

T 6: *You mean ask her if she wants to work with the class, or do it somewhere else?*

C 6: *Yes. There's a room here where she could be alone, but be observable by others.*

Ms. Rhodes agreed that talking with the child when both were calm might bring to light why Christy was so angry, and an interview with the counselor also was arranged. The teacher decided that a talk with the child's mother might reveal some difficulty that Christy was having at home, and perhaps taking out on the teacher in the classroom. She also determined to handle future occurrences of this kind by refusing to allow herself to show hurt, but withdrawing from a struggle of power, especially by giving Christy choices in a friendly way.

Authors' Comments and Discussion Questions

In this case the consultant is presented with a situation in which the child is refusing to cooperate with the teacher. The teacher brings a letter that provoked strong feelings in the teacher, but at C1 the consultant does not investigate these feelings. Instead the consultant explores the sequence of events.

1. What is your reaction to the consultant's failure to immediately acknowledge and explore the teacher's feeling? How might this affect the teacher?

2. How else might the consultant have responded at C3? How could the consultant also explore the relevant components of the child's motivation? What do you think about the consultant's response at C4? Discuss this in light of the T4 response and indicate how you could continue to explore the situation.

3. At C6 the consultant was still not dealing with the teacher's feelings in posing a solution. Discuss the dynamics and other procedures to use in the interview.

CASE 4
JOYCE AND MRS. BLAKE

Authors' Introductory Comment

This case describes one of the living environments in which many of today's children and youths are being nurtured. The consultant did not let his emotions get in the way and dealt with the teacher's problem rather that rationalizing or complaining about the terrible home situation.

Consultee

Mrs. Blake is an eighth grade English teacher now beginning her sixth year of teaching. She is a graduate of a state teachers' college and has done additional work toward a degree in English.

Presenting Problem

Joyce is a thirteen-year-old girl who has experienced severe emotional problems in school. Teachers' comments in her cumulative record include such statements as *"Joyce is so moody —her emotional states are so extreme,"* and *"Joyce seems to be forever crying about something—I never seem to know why."* Joyce does not get along with the other kids and is deeply hurt by teasing comments. Her teachers say she is very demanding of their time and attention, always "hanging around" the desk.

Family Atmosphere

Joyce has always lived with her maternal grandparents. She was born when her mother was seventeen and was taken by her grandmother shortly thereafter. Her mother later married and has two sons whom Joyce resents. Despite the fact that Joyce's mother has maintained frequent contact with Joyce and her grandparents, the grandparents make all the decisions in regard to Joyce's upbringing. Joyce's grandfather is a retired railroad worker whose main income is a small pension. Both grandparents are conservative and strict in their demands on Joyce. They live in a rural and remote section of the country.

Family Constellation

Robert and Joe are half brothers whom Joyce sees frequently. They are both of primary school age.

Joyce is in eighth grade and attends a rural elementary school that is currently involved in some programs to improve its curriculum.

Approach to Problem

The consultant began individual consulting sessions with Mrs. Blake.

C 1: *You wanted to talk to me about Joyce—what seems to be the difficulty?*

T 1: *I don't know what to do with her. She seems to be forever looking for ways to get her feelings hurt.*

C 2: *You mean that she seems to want to be hurt?*

T 2: *Sort of. The things that have no effect on the other students seem to be devastating to Joyce.*

C 3: *What kind of things?*

T 3: *Oh, you know, a reprimand for any minor thing, like interrupting. She is always interrupting me or the other students.*

C 4: *She seems to need all the attention?*

T 4: *Yes, in any way she can, she gets it.*

C 5: *If she can't get some positive reaction, she'll settle for a negative one?*

T 5: *Yes, I know she can anticipate my reactions; she is bright enough to know full well what things are irritating to me, but she does them anyway.*

C 6: *Why do you think Joyce has to be in the limelight all the time?*

T 6: *Well, I know she has lots of problems at home. She has a very unfortunate home situation. Do you know about that?*

C 7: *You mean the fact that she doesn't live with her mother?*

T 7: *Yes, plus the fact that she wants to, and her mother does not seem interested in taking her.*

C 8: *I guess that would seem to be the supreme rejection. She probably feels that if her Mother doesn't want her she must be quite unlovable.*

T 8: *I guess in a way that's what she's trying to prove all the time. She somehow equates attention with acceptance. She simply cannot stand to be ignored. Even if what she does really makes her more rejected at times.*

C 9: *You think then that she just doesn't know how to go about finding positive ways of being noticed and accepted?*

T 9: *Yes, that was why I wanted you to begin seeing her; maybe you could help her gain some insight into her behavior.*

C10: *Okay, but in the meantime, what do you think could be done to create acceptance in the classroom—like, how could you head her off before she resorts to bickering and sulking to get attention?*

T10: *I don't know. She writes very well, maybe we could capitalize on that.*

C11: *Possibly have her do something on a continuing basis that she might like to share with the group?*

T11: *I'll work on that; I know the idea will have some appeal to her.*

C12: *Keep me posted on your progress. I'll be interested to know how she responds to your suggestions.*

Results and Conclusions

The most interesting aspect of this particular case was that Joyce became very involved in what she called her "novel." She wrote regularly about a fictitious girl who exhibited many of the anxieties and frustrations that she herself encountered in living. Other members of her class became interested in her writing and often made suggestions for events to take place in her story. Joyce was able to find an outlet for her feelings and at the same time was forming positive relationships with the other students and her teacher.

Only a few weeks after the initial consultations took place, Joyce's teachers began to comment on the change in her attitude. She seemed happier, and the outbursts that had been so frequent had disappeared. A sociogram administered at the end of the semester indicated that Joyce's acceptance with the group had improved markedly.

Authors' Comments and Discussion Questions

1. At T5 we can see how negative attention is acceptable. At C6 the consultant responds in a most appropriate fashion to the real issue. How is this done?

2. At C9 the problem seems to be a learning problem. How would you teach the missing skills?

3. Was the plan of action detailed enough? Do vague plans of action work?

4. Do you have any suggestions about how the consultant could have responded or behaved differently?

CASE 5
WILLIE B AND MR. AARON

Authors' Introductory Comment

The high school milieu is a difficult arena in which to work as a consultant. Students, teachers, and parents are in many cases already deeply discouraged by this stage. Consulting, however, can and does work at this level and should perhaps be the preferred mode of treatment.

Presenting Problem

Mr. Aaron, a 30-year-old high school math teacher, is now in his sixth year of teaching high school mathematics. He holds a bachelor's degree from a large urban teacher training university and has since added courses towards a master's degree in mathematics.

Willie B. is a 17-year-old male who has a long history of school behavior difficulties and of poor achievement. He is a loner in class and often appears to behave in a bizarre manner that is sure to gain him the complete attention of the class or teacher.

Family Atmosphere

Willie lives at home with his mother, three sisters, and younger brother. Two older sisters have been out of the home for two years. His father lived with the family until Willie was 12 years old but has since separated from Willie's mother.

Willie's mother often works long hours and is the sole supporter of the family. She has a health problem and is sometimes unable to work.

Willie's maternal grandparents, who were part of the home before his parents separated, have since died. When his mother is working, the children are without adult supervision in the morning and after school. During the evening hours, the mother must rest a great deal and appears to be only interested in knowing where the children are and keeping them quiet.

Family Constellation

Deborah (21 years old), a high school graduate, is currently married and the mother of two young sons.

Priscilla (20 years old) dropped out of school when she became pregnant and is now married, living away from home.

Teri (19 years old) graduated from high school but is still employed and living at home.

Willie (17 years old) is the fourth sibling. He is currently in a special education program designed for slow learners. The high school in which Willie is a third-year student is located in an inner-city community. While the school generally follows the traditional approach to the educative process, changes are occurring and new approaches are being tried, at least in some individual instances.

Walter (12 years old) is Willie's younger brother.

Discussion Questions

Without reading further, what is your plan of action? With whom would you work in this situation?

Authors' Note

The purpose of behavior seems to be more than attention. If attention were the payoff, Willie would stop when he received it. Instead he continues in an effort to show he is boss or to hurt others.

Approach to Problem

The consultant suggested individual consulting sessions when Mr. Aaron sent a referral slip on the student, Willie B.

C 1: *Before I meet with Willie, why don't we talk about the problem that is so disturbing to you?*

T 1: *I didn't want to write out a referral slip, but I am not getting anywhere with Willie since he was placed in my math class.*

C 2: *What seems to be happening in the class?*

T 2: (Teacher describes incidents occurring in class).

After some general observations, the discussion focuses on specific student-teacher relationships.

C 3: *Do you have any ideas about what prompts Willie to act as he does?*

T 3: *I have thought about that a great deal, and while I feel it's surely to gain attention, it also seems to be more than that.*

C 4: *By "more than that" do you mean that Willie is aware of what he is doing when he behaves as he does?*

T 4: *No, I guess not. But sometimes I can't help feeling that Willie knows just how to get my goat and does just that.*

C 5: *Well, have you tried anything that seems to work well with Willie?*

T 5: *Nothing I try seems to last very long. But sometimes talking to him calmly and giving him my assurance and extra time to talk things out seems to work fairly well, at the time.*

C 6: *What else could you do to help the situation?*

T 6: *I guess I could find out if there is really a physical basis for some of Willie's behavior. The kids all say he is having a fit.*

C 7: *But, what could you personally do in the classroom situation to help relieve Willie's need for complete attention regardless of cause?*

T 7: (uncomfortable silence)

C 8: *Well, would you be willing to try a new approach to the situation? What if every time Willie acted up, you would take some concrete action instead of trying to ignore the behavior or making idle threats that aren't followed up?*

T 8: *Like what?*

C 9: *It's clear that Willie's behavior often keeps the class from their work. Suppose you gave Willie the choice at that time either to work with the class or take his assignment and work in the library until he is ready to cooperate?*

T 9: *He may be spending more time in the library than in class that way.*

C10: *Well, is he or the class getting anything out of his remaining there when he acts as he does?*

T10: *No. I guess you're right.*

C11: *Perhaps, the day Willie is in the library, the class as a whole could discuss the problem Willie presents to the class and offer their suggestions as to how they could deal with it.*

T11: *That sounds good; I'll try it.*

C12: *And, as you said Willie responds to a calm speaking voice when you give him your personal reassurance, let this be your guide in dealing with him. Act firmly, don't lose your cool, and continually let Willie know that you are concerned with him as a person, not merely with his outward behavior.*

T12: *Well, it won't hurt to try.*

C13: *Good! How will you go about it?*

T13: *If Willie acts up in class tomorrow, then I won't spend class time warning him to stop or get all steamed up inside by trying to ignore his actions, but I'll act right away instead by letting him know very calmly that his behavior is not acceptable to the class. He can either choose to be a part of the class or he can take his work to the library until he is ready to be with the class.*

T14: *You might speak to Willie privately during your personal period to reassure him of your interest and help prepare him for this new role of decision making on his part.*

C15: *Fine. Can we meet at this same time next week to see how well this works?*

T15: *All right. This may not work, but at least it's a start.*

Results and Conclusions

The teacher met with the consultant for several weeks regularly and then on occasion as the situation warranted. An additional session with the teacher, the nurse, and the parent did uncover a physical as well as emotional cause for Willie's behavior. Through their efforts a determination was made that Willie had shown petit mal symptoms for some time (some of his bizarre behavior was, in fact, the result of mild seizures), and as a result of these consultations, Willie had begun treatment at a nearby hospital.

At the end of the school term, Willie was working cooperatively with the class, with only an occasional need to work in the library. His mathematics skills were improved enough to allow him to pass on with the rest of the class, and while his attention-seeking behavior does crop up from time to time, he appears to be much more in control of his action at this time.

With the help of his teacher and counselor, Willie was encouraged to enter into the total school program and, as a result, he is no longer a loner. While the teacher discontinued the consultation after Willie moved on, he continued to seek help and encouragement from the consultant from time to time in regard to new approaches he wished to undertake with other students presenting problems in his class.

Authors' Comments and Discussion Questions

1. At T1 the teacher implies that the consultant is responsible for the problem with Willie. How would you deal with this statement?

2. At T4 the teacher makes a significant disclosure. He begins to relate his role in the interpersonal conflict with Willie. How might the consultant have focused on this and clarified it for Willie?

3. Are you sure about what the teacher does in T5 that works with Willie? How would you request further clarification?

4. The consultant seems interested in finding a solution or solving the problem before understanding the child's goal or payoff. Is it advisable to do this; to work out a solution before the problem is clarified?

5. At C13 the consultant makes sure that the consultee knows exactly what it is he will do. Why is this done?

CASE 6
KERRY AND MRS. SALE

Authors' Introductory Comment

In this case the teacher presents a difficult nine-year-old child who delights in doing the opposite of instructions. The consultant is able to generate several recommendations for Mrs. Sale.

Consultee

Mrs. Sale is a college graduate beginning her first year of teaching in an ungraded, innovative system that includes children ages six to nine. Mrs. Sale has a homeroom of eight-year-olds and reading and math classes of mixed ages and abilities.

Presenting Problem

Kerry is a nine-year-old child who had been displaying some rather violent tendencies such as kicking, hitting, and fighting other children; writing hate letters; refusing to produce assignments; and demanding a great deal of teacher attention. She also made up fantasy stories about exotic trips and one concerning her father dying from a serious disease.

Family Constellation

Jeffrey, 14 years old

Carol, 13 years old

Anne, 12 years old

Jonathan, 10 years old

Kerry, 9 years old

Scott, 8 years old

Kerry is flanked by a younger and older brother, while two older sisters follow one another in the family constellation. Kerry is near the end of the family, but is not the baby.

Teacher Anecdotes and Specific Incidents

Incident #1

Context: Reading lesson

Child's Action: Hits child as result of a remark.

Teacher's Action: Surprise, stops lesson, scolds Kerry and others.

Child's Response: Obvious satisfaction.

Purpose: Revenge(?)

Incident #2

Context: Reading lesson

Child's Action: Refuses to do work sheet.

Teacher's Action: Teacher urges her to begin.

Child's Response: "Hate stare" pouts.

Purpose: Attention, power over teacher.

Incident #3

Context: Reading lesson

Child's Action: Comes late and refuses to take test the other children have begun.

Teacher's Action: Tells her to do anything, but to keep quiet.

Child's Response: Folds arms, then begins to draw.

Purpose: Attention, power.

Incident #4

Context: Homeroom

Child's Action: Writes hate letter to the teacher.

Teacher's Action: Ignores.

Child's Response: Continues writing.

Purpose: Keeps teacher's attention.

Incident #5

Context: Social Studies

Child's Action: Fictitious travel story, Kerry's voice becomes high and dreamy.

Teacher's Action: Acknowledges contribution but not story.

Child's Response: Sits down.

Purpose: Attention.

Approach to Problem

Of immediate concern to the teacher were the outbursts of anger and violent attacks on the other children.

T 1: *Something has got to be done with Kerry.*

C 1: *Could you explain a little more, you sound quite frustrated.*

T 2: *Yes, this violence to other children has just got to stop before someone else gets hurt.*

C 2: *Someone already has?*

T 3: *I'm afraid so. Yesterday two girls began accusing Kerry of being kicked out of a club they belong to and before I even realized what was happening, Kerry had hit one of them on the side of the face, leaving quite a welt. Today she was supposedly "hired" by two girls to fight a third one they thought had taken some money from them.*

C 3: *How did you feel at the time the first incident was taking place?*

T 4: *Really angry and annoyed. I felt like I wanted to side with the girl who was hit, even though she did provoke Kerry. But Kerry's reactions are always overreactions, out of proportion to the occasion. She has quite a temper.*

C 4: *Do you have any ideas as to what results her temper brings about?*

T 5: *I'm not sure I follow you.*

C 5: *Well, think of it this way; what is the purpose of her temper?*

T 6: Well yes, all eyes are fixed on Kerry; she has our attention, that's for sure!!

C 6: *Exactly—just what she wants.*

T 7: *So now what do I do?*

C 7: *Perhaps we could think of some way of defusing her.*

T 8: *You mean, find some way of getting to her before she...*

C 8: *Yes, what would you think of letting her take a five minute "time-out" occasionally when you see signs building up. Speak to her firmly but not angrily, and explain that she may come back before that if she's ready. She also may ask to leave herself, rather than you asking her to; that way she will be aware of her responsibility in the matter also. Perhaps you also could call attention to those times she is thoughtful of other children in the class, or asks to help a child who is slower in reading than she is.*

T 9: *Well, it's worth a try.*

C 9: *Let's do it for a week, and I'll check with you next Thursday to see how you and she and the class are doing.*

Along with individual counseling, Kerry began to get the attention she needed, and in less than three weeks, the violence was reduced. However, she still would refuse to cooperate in other areas, partially as a result of having her own way, that is, controlling people for so long. Her teacher again returned for help in coping with this aspect of the problem.

T10: *Kerry came into reading class today and refused to take the test the other children had already begun. She said she was stupid and should not really be in this group and demanded to be moved to another room, adding that I didn't like her anyway.*

C10: *How did you react?*

T11: *I told her I didn't care what she did, only to keep quiet since the children were taking the test. But I know I shouldn't have said I didn't care, because I do — but sometimes...*

C11: *She gets you cornered?*

T12: *Yes, but I know giving in to her and moving her, even though it sure would be peaceful for me, would only convince Kerry that I really agreed she is stupid.*

C12: *It seems to me that Kerry is actually a very smart little girl to devise that way of demanding your attention, and getting out of something unpleasant.*

T13: *You said it!!*

C13: *Have you ever thought of mentioning that to Kerry? With perhaps a knowing smile?*

C14: *Instead of engaging in a battle of words with her, why don't you try this? Do you have any corrected reading workbook pages that need to be returned to children?*

T15: *Yes, plenty.*

C15: *Who usually gives them out?*

T16: *Sometimes I do, sometimes someone who's finished with the work.*

C16: *All right, hold one set back. When Kerry stages a scene, instead of getting involved, why not try saying, "Oh, Kerry, you reminded me, these papers need to be given out. Would you do that for me?" I have a hunch she will jump at the chance. You will have turned the tables on her and given her an opportunity to absorb some healthy attention.*

Results and Conclusions

This recommendation did work. The consultant and teacher also found a permanent job for Kerry; one that satisfied her need for attention and gave her a sense of responsibility. Kerry began collecting the attendance sheets from the primary grades every afternoon. Kerry has a long way to go but progress is evident, and even Kerry is aware of it herself.

Authors' Comments and Discussion Questions

In this incident a teacher presented a situation in which the child was demanding attention and at times refusing to cooperate. Although the consultant had collected family atmosphere and family constellation data, there seemed to be little utilization of it.

1. What information about the family atmosphere and constellation would suggest some tentative hypotheses about this behavior?

2. Although the dialogue with the teacher usually discussed Kerry's purpose as attention, what other possible purposes do you see? How would these purposes be "checked out" with the teacher?

3. Assuming you identified other purposes, indicate how you would handle the interview and formulation of recommendations.

4. In the first interview at T4 response, we have a clue as to the purpose of Kerry's behavior. How might the consultant have responded differently in C4?

5. At C6 how could the consultant have kept the exploration more open?

6. In the second teacher interview, what alternative responses could the consultant make at C2?

The consultant in a limited time period helped facilitate a number of solutions but perhaps generated too many hypotheses and recommendations in contrast to encouraging the teacher to collaborate in that role.

CASE 7
JIMMY: A CASE OF TEACHER-PARENT COOPERATION

Authors' Introductory Comment

When parents and teachers cooperate, the chances of helping children increase. This case describes how rather simple "problems" can be indicative of a total life-style and how, once identified, they can be modified quickly and effectively when home and school work together.

Presenting Problem

Jimmy is a five-year-old boy who does very little in the classroom unless the teacher is with him. He chooses the same activity, a puzzle, each day at activity time, does not socialize with the other children, and does not put his own sweater on at dismissal.

Family Atmosphere

Jimmy lives at home with his mother and father and is the only child. His mother is home all day and does everything for Jimmy. When the father is home, he does the household chores and expects nothing from his son. If anything is expected of Jimmy, it is always with one or both parents supervising the activities.

Jimmy did not attend any preschools; kindergarten is his first school experience. Early in the school year the teacher noticed problems with this child. He seemed to not follow directions, but was not oppositional or defiant. At first the teacher was concerned about a hearing loss, but screening ruled out this explanation.

When the teacher focused her attention on Jimmy, he did respond and could do the work. The teacher had to stay with Jimmy to help him complete his work. He was a student that took a disproportionate amount of time, was not a discipline problem, but fell behind if he did not get this attention.

One day the teacher asked the class to do worksheets individually. She noticed Jimmy staring into space and not doing his work; she then went over to his desk and worked with him for several minutes. When the teacher moved to another child, Jimmy stopped and watched her. He did not speak to any of the children although interaction was going on around him. At the end of the period Jimmy stood up and waited helplessly, and the girl next to him helped him to finish the puzzle so that he could put it away.

At another time, during a school fire drill, the consultant observed the teacher returning through the moving lines of children and holding Jimmy by the hand, taking him to his place with the class.

Teacher Consultation

Since Jimmy appeared to be receiving special attention by playing helpless, the consultant suggested that Jimmy be placed at a table with children who were sociable so that Jimmy might be encouraged to interact with them; also to find things that Jimmy could do; and to refuse to help him with the things he could already do—such as putting on his sweater. An appointment was set up for the consultant to meet with the mother.

Mother Consultation

The mother began the consultation session by saying that the teacher was concerned that Jimmy did not listen and follow directions in class. The consultant clarified the purpose of the session by stating that he was working with the teacher in the classroom situation and wondered if the mother was concerned about anything at home with Jimmy. The consultant suggested that the mother begin by telling about a typical day at home. The mother told how she dressed Jimmy, waited on him, and continually reprimanded and nagged him to hurry. In her exasperation she usually ended up doing most of the things that Jimmy could have done.

The consultant discussed the faulty goal of the child —getting special service and attention by playing helpless. The unfairness to the mother also was discussed because it required her to be always available for service. (She was even picking him up at school and putting on his coat for him.) The mother decided to be less available. She would put out his clothes for him and he was to dress himself and be dressed in order to have breakfast.

She would not get involved in power struggles with him about picking up his things and would refrain from telling him things that he already knew. Up to this time Jimmy had no need to listen; all he had to do was stand there and eventually his mother would do it. He had no need to communicate with her verbally. She mentioned that Jimmy liked to read. The consultant made this known to the teacher.

Teacher Consultation--Second

The teacher had requested that the children around Jimmy not help him get dressed or do things for him. She got Jimmy to read some stories to other children and asked him to help with their alphabet cards. Jimmy has seemed to improve after this. He is now volunteering to answer in the group and is managing to get himself dressed. The teacher is pleased with his progress.

Mother Consultation--Second

M 1: *When he got up I laid his clothes out, and I said, "Jimmy, here are your clothes. When you get your clothes on, come to the kitchen and I'll give you breakfast." So he looked at me kind of funny—(laughter) so I said "Go on, get started and get your clothes on." and I just walked away from him. So I went back to the kitchen and left him by himself. Well, he got into his underclothes and then he came back to the kitchen and I said, "you don't have your pants on or your shirt." So he stood there a while and he looked at me, you know, and I said, "go back and get your shirt and your pants and get them on." So he turned around slowly and went back to his room and about 15 or 20 minutes later he came back to the kitchen and he had them on. (Laughter)*

C 1: *How did you feel when that happened?*

M 2: *I felt like I had made a great big accomplishment.*

C 2: *And then what happened?*

M 3: *Well, he came and had his breakfast.*

C 3: *What happened the next morning?*

M 4: *The next two days my husband was home and his father felt that he should help him.*

C 4: *I wonder if there would be any chance of meeting with both of you sometime?*

An appointment was set up for both parents.......

C 5: *How are things going for him?*

M 5: *Well, I was up in the classroom now. I help the teacher two days a week, and I noticed that he doesn't listen too well.* (She explained the incident.)

C 6: *Do you know why he wasn't listening?*

M 6: *His mind seemed to have been somewhere else.*

C 7: *I wonder if he ever has to listen, if there is any need for him to listen.*

M 7: *Well, sometimes I feel that he thinks he doesn't have to listen.*

C 8: *He probably doesn't need to listen. All he has to do is just stand there and it will be taken care of.* (Pause) *You know, the same thing as you telling him over and over to hurry up and get dressed. He doesn't have to listen because what does he know will happen?*

M 8: (Laughs) *That I'll dress him.*

C 9: *Right, you'll step right in and do it...do you notice this happening at home—not listening?*

M 9: *Yes, you have to tell him to do something more than once. He hears but the point is that he doesn't want to do it then and there.*

C10: *Another thing that is happening, sometimes we talk too much, instead of acting, so that kids become mother-deaf and teacher-deaf. Can you think of a particular time when this happened at home, when you told him over and over?*

M10: *I told him last week about the puzzle that he built on the floor, and I had to tell him over and over to pick it up.*

C11: *What would have happened if you had not told him to pick it up?*

M11: *Well, usually he does pick up his things and put them away without being told. But this one time he just didn't want to do it. He looked at me and I said, "Go on and pick it up." and he started picking up one piece at a time.*

C12: *Real slowly?*

M12: *Yes, real slowly.*

C13: *How did you feel when he did that?*

M13: *I felt impatient and felt like shaking him and making him do it.*

C14: *That is the reason why he was doing that, it was like a little power struggle—you told him to do something and he wasn't going to do it. You wanted your way and he wanted his way. I wonder what would have happened if you had left the puzzle there.*

M14: *Eventually I think he would have picked it up by himself, because he usually takes very good care of his things.*

C15: *Do you think this was something you were expecting too soon from him?*

M15: *That could have been.*

C16: *That's a strong point. The fact that he is good about taking care of his things. Do you mention that to him sometimes?*

M16: *No, I don't think I have.*

C17: *It might be a way to encourage him, just by noticing something like that, a way of giving him some positive kinds of attention for the things that he can do. You might surprise him sometimes by noticing things that he does that you like and then he wouldn't have to feel that he has to get your attention by doing things that you don't like, that are annoying to you. These are ways of encouraging him and giving him a sense that he can do things and be of help.*

Results and Conclusions

An appointment was set up for both parents, but the next week only the mother came. At this time the mother told the consultant that Jimmy has made some definite changes at home —now he likes to dress himself and is proud when he does it. Jimmy even demanded that his Dad let him do it himself. Jimmy was showing more initiative in doing things for himself such as getting food from the refrigerator. The mother was pleased with Jimmy's progress.

Authors' Comments and Discussion Questions

1. At M4 a common situation is brought out — that of parents working at cross purposes. At C4 the consultant offers his help to get the parents working together. Is this necessary? Should consultants be involved with couple counseling?

2. At C8 the consultant makes a guess that leads to insight at M8. Is it OK for consultants to take chances like this? Isn't this manipulation? What if the consultant is wrong?

3.The consultant is confronting the mother in a very helpful fashion at C10. He is also gathering specific incidents in order to understand the same problem that the consultee sees.

4.At C13 and M13 the consultant is attempting to discover the goal of Jimmy's behavior through understanding his mother's feelings to his action. What is Jimmy's goal?

5.At M14 we can see how the mother was previously acting on an irrational belief. She stated that her son was usually responsible yet she treated him as though he were irresponsible. What does the consultant do when discrepancies such as these are uncovered?

6.At C16 the consultant identifies something good that the child is doing and encourages the consultee to notice this behavior. This is usually the most important part in behavior modification programs—encouraging the positive—not just removing the negative.

INDEX

INDEX

major theoretical concepts 225-227

model for 223

Feedback 190, *Figure* 188

promoting 202, *Figure* 199

Feelings 65

adequacy 43-45

failure 43-45

Festinger, L. 20, 24

Fink, 178

Forces

acceptance 186-187

altruism 1919-192

encourage 192-193

feedback 190

interaction 192

reality testing 191

spectator learning 190

therapeutic 186-193

therapeutic in parent groups 218-219

universalization 191

ventilation 187

Frame of reference

external 54

internal 56

Fuqua, F. 107, 122

G

Gerler, E.R. 174, 204

Gibbs, J.T. 49, 51

Glasser, W. 44, 51

Glenn, S. 136, 169

Goals 65, 185

aligned 179

created 70

disclosure 201, *Figure* 198

misbehavior 64, 65, *Figures* 66-67, 68-69

subjective 70

therapeutic process 228-230

unconscious 70

Goals of teen

misbehavior 65, *Figure* 68-69

Gray, L. 77, 86

Group

See Groups

C group 143-152

interaction principles 181-183

norms 185

organizing the C 144-148

parent C 216-218

prestige of member 185

stages 215-216

understanding 181-186

Group dynamics 183-186

Group skills

leading the classroom 193, 196-197

Groups

learning cycle 214-218

parent education 214-218

problem-solving 140-142

rationale 140-142

therapeutic forces in 186-193, 218-219

working with 139-140

Grunwald, B. 196, 204

Guidelines

consultation 3-5

Gutkin, T.B. 14, 25

H

Hansen, J.C. 20, 24

Hawes, D. 37, 51

Helpers

effective 104-105

Heredity 55

Himes, B.S. 20, 24

Holloway, E.L. 13, 25, 27, 28, 52

Human behavior

theory of 138

Human potential 32

Humanness

factors that block 179-181

Humoring 38

Hypotheses 16, 25

I

I-Messages 82, 139, *Figure* 84

Idiographic nature 74

In-service

components 135-138

essential topics 138-140

Individual psychology 2, 56

goal-directed approach 2

Information

ABOUT
THE
AUTHORS

Dr. Don Dinkmeyer, Jr., Ph.D., is an Associate Professor of Counseling in the Graduate College of Western Kentucky University. He is co-author of educational materials such as STEP parent education program, "The Next STEP," and the childcare professionals training program "Teaching and Leading Children."

Dinkmeyer has been a school and mental health counselor, and has trained helping professionals across North America for more than 18 years. He has worked with the United States Navy, psychiatric hospitals, and many other facilities. His work includes consultations with Parents Anonymous, the Connecticut Coalition Against Domestic Violence, and numerous elementary, middle, and high school settings.

Dinkmeyer has served two terms as President of the North American Society of Adlerian Psychology and has co-authored two editions of the textbook *Adlerian Counseling and Psychotherapy*. He has served the Office of Substance Abuse Prevention (OSAP) as an invited member of the OSAP parent education task force.

Don lives in Bowling Green, Kentucky with his wife, two stepsons, and daughter. They currently span the age range of teen to preschooler.

Jon Carlson, Psy.D., Ed.D., is a Distinguished Professor of Psychology and Counseling at Governors State University, University Park, Illinois, and a psychologist in Lake Geneva, Wisconsin. In addition, he has served as the school counselor/psychologist at the Woods School in Lake Geneva for 15 years. Dr Carlson is a Fellow of the American Psychological Association, a Diplomate in Family Psychology of the American Board of Professional Psychology, and holds a certificate in psychotherapy from the Alfred Adler Institute in Chicago.

Dr. Carlson has authored 15 books, 100 professional articles, and is the editor of *Individual Psychology: The Journal of Adlerian Theory, Research, and Practice*; and *The Family Journal*.

He has received national awards for his contributions from NASAP, ACA, IAMFC, APA, and Chi Sigma Iota.

He and his wife are parents of 5 children.

Don Dinkmeyer, Sr., Ph.D., is president of Communication & Motivation Training Institute, Coral Springs, Florida, and a psychologist in private practice. He received an honorary Doctor of Letters from Concordia University in Illinois. He holds Diplomates in Counseling Psychology and Family Psychology from the American Board of Professional Psychology and a Diplomate in Marital and Family Therapy, from the American Board of Family Psychology.

He has taught on the elementary, high school, and university levels. Dr. Dinkmeyer is a Fellow of the American Psychological Association.

He is the recipient of the American Association for Counseling and Development (AACD) Professional Award, and the Mace Medal from the Association for Couples in Marriage Enrichment (ACME).

He received the North American Society of Adlerian Psychology award for contributions to Adlerian Psychology, and was selected as a Distinguished Senior Contributor to Counseling Psychology by APA.

He originated the *Elementary School Guidance and Counseling Journal*, an ACA publication. He is a member of the *USA Today* Permanent Parenting Panel.

Dr. Dinkmeyer has collaborated on a number of programs that have been widely used in educational circles. These programs include *Developing Understanding of Self and Others (DUSO), Systematic Training for Effective Parenting (STEP), STEP/Teen, Next STEP, Early Childhood STEP, PREP for Effective Family Living, TIME for a Better Marriage, Systematic Training for Effective Teaching (STET), and Teaching and Leading Children (TLC).*

He is the author of 28 books and more than 150 professional articles. Among some popular co-authored books are *The Encouragement Book, Adlerian Counseling & Psychotherapy, Systems of Family Therapy, Raising a Responsible Child, New Beginnings,* and *Leadership by Encouragement.* Booklets include *Basics of Adult/Teen Relationships, Basics of Self Acceptance, Basics of Marriage,* and *Basics of Understanding Your Lifestyle.*

Dr. Dinkmeyer has consulted and conducted workshops in 46 states, Canada, Mexico, South America, Japan, England, and Europe.